Sambo

An Essential Guide to a Martial Art Similar to Judo, Jiu-Jitsu, and Wrestling along with Its Throws, Grappling Styles, Holds, and Submission Techniques

Table of Contents

Introduction

Sambo is a martial art resembling the discipline of Judo but with some variations. In this book, you'll learn basic terminology and techniques on throws, grip techniques, self-defense moves in Sambo, offensive rolls, and strikes - even ways to improve your skills at this exciting sport.

Sambo is a Russian martial art; its name is an acronym meaning "self-defense without weapons." It was initially developed in the 1900s to provide unarmed combat training for the Soviet military. It is very similar to Judo, jiu-jitsu, and wrestling but has many unique aspects.

Sambo, although derived from Judo, has unique technical differences. Since the art form was initially developed for the military, Sambo inherently has a lot of combat elements. For example, Combat Sambo allows more aggressive maneuvers of strikes, elbow, knee kicks, etc. Sambo Masters do very well in Mixed Martial Arts (MMA) competitions – thanks to the martial art's versatility.

Mastering Sambo reaps many benefits for those who train in it. Firstly, Sambo is great for self-defense since the techniques are practical and efficient. Furthermore, this martial art is excellent for fitness and self-improvement. Sambo requires a lot of strength to perform throws against stronger opponents, ultimately building endurance.

Sambo has a variety of throwing techniques. There are throws to take your opponent down if they are standing, sitting, or lying down. The grips used in Sambo allow for many combinations and attacks on your opponent – so practicing them is very beneficial.

Sambo also has many grip fighting techniques which can be used to gain an advantage during a match. Depending on the situation, you can also use your hands or legs, and these moves allow you to control your opponent effectively.

Mastering Sambo requires diligent practice and training over many years. Becoming an expert Sambo practitioner is not easy, but the benefits are worth it.

This encyclopedia-style manual is a must-have for Sambo fighters of all levels. It contains everything from the history to grip techniques, submissions, and self-defense in a clear, concise format perfect for beginners looking to become experts or executives who want to take up the sport.

Putting the self-defense techniques in context makes this book an easy-to-follow guide that equips readers with the essential information they need to gain mastery over this martial art. No details are left out from Chapter 1: What Is Sambo? to Chapter 10: Improving Your Sambo Skills.

This essential guide introduces different throws and rolls and self-defense. Tap into our expertise.

In this Sambo guide, you learn the fundamental elements of Sambo. There's much for readers to learn, with detailed sections on throws and holding techniques, headlocks and chokes, arm locks, and pins. Look closer at the different styles of wrestling applied in Sambo, including Judo, Brazilian Jiu-Jitsu, and Wrestling Systems, which make up a larger percentage of all competitions worldwide.

Most books on this topic are theoretical surveys covering basic information about techniques, strategies, and observations without providing anything specific for one person's needs. This guide gives you all the raw knowledge to learn the basics through hands-on training with an experienced instructor. The book also gives detailed guidance on solo drills for self-practice.

You'll be walked through each step, from carefully explained procedures for moves like pins or throws to descriptions of style changes, position shifts, and general positions –providing clear instructions on how these transitions should be made.

Chapter 1: What Is Sambo?

Over the years, more people have become interested in learning martial arts. It's everyone's top priority to ensure their safety and mental and physical health. Luckily, nothing combines self-defense, physical strength and health, and mental well-being and stimulation like the practice of martial arts.

You might be surprised to learn there are over 170 martial arts. China, Japan, and Korea are known for being the ancestral homelands of various combating and self-defense techniques such as Karate, Jiu-Jitsu, and Taekwondo. However, Sambo is a renowned Russian sport.

Sambo was created as a universal combat system. Aficionados worked tirelessly to collect, select, and seamlessly combine a wide array of elements as a foundation for the universal combat sport that is Sambo. The sport's teaching programs are highly distinctive, making its practitioners masterful in numerous techniques and skillful in tactical thinking, as needed on the mat.

The acronym SAMBO derives from the phrase "Samooborona Bez Oruzhia," which translates into "Self Defense Without Weapons." It is structured based on defense rather than attack, which comes in handy in several situations we face in today's world.

Aside from teaching invaluable self-defense techniques, Sambo can help individuals build strong character. It teaches perseverance and endurance, qualities we need to make indispensable life experiences and withstand their complexities.

Not only does Sambo help us guard ourselves against potential predators, but it also helps us stay safe during other everyday incidents. For instance, slip and fall accidents are among the most common reasons for injuries. Whether you twist your ankle while walking or slip on a wet surface, you can stay safe by employing the Sambo fall technique. A safe fall technique is a must-learn for any wrestling system.

This sport teaches countless incredible qualities and traits. It is about physical strength and is also concerned with producing strong-willed individuals. Sambo helps individuals develop important character traits such as self-discipline, control, diligence, persistence, and will. These character aspects can heighten a sense of self-awareness outside the training facility.

For some, Sambo is their fuel, even if they view it as a professional sport. Others think of Sambo as a hobby and a way to work on self-growth and development. Regardless of what this sport means to you, it can be an awesome complementary addition to your career. It can serve as a stress outlet, a timeout, or the perfect opportunity to get your creative juices flowing.

This book is perfect if you're considering giving Sambo a go. We delve deep into what Sambo is and where it derived from throughout this chapter. There is no better way to start your journey than understanding the sport and its history you're getting into. Some Sambo subtypes are covered, and the differences between them are explained.

Getting to Know Sambo

So, what is Sambo? Sambo is a Soviet combat sport and martial art. As mentioned, it is an acronym of a Romanized Russian phrase meaning self-defense without weapons. It is among the newest or most modern martial art forms. According to United World Wrestling, it is acknowledged as the third most popular international wrestling style.

It was initially created for the military to aid in ending fights as efficiently and quickly as possible. Not long after, Sambo became an international competitive sport.

Judo, Jujitsu, and other martial arts forms inspired Sambo's make-up, movements, and techniques. This collection of wrestling or combat systems is widely known as a *self-defense art.*

In Sambo, like other wrestling systems, the fighters must comply with specific regulations and rules. The fight involves two individuals who employ different tricks and blows. The points earned are an evaluation of their tricks, and, of course, the wrestler with the highest number of points wins. The match can be ended before its allotted time limit if a player successfully attempts various submission tricks and locks on their opponent.

As you have realized, this sport is not easy to grasp. Therefore, Sambo wrestlers must undergo rigorous training to acquire the needed skills and techniques. Wrestlers should be able to grapple and strike in the clinch.

Although Sambo is a defense sport, it still requires aggressive play, especially during matches. Success during the match depends on acquiring and mastering a wide range of skills.

Flexibility and agility are required for joint locks, throws, suffocation techniques, kicks, and strikes. These are skills and moves that must be tactfully used throughout the match.

To learn Sambo, you must understand it takes years of practice and dedication to master the art. It is not a sport for those lacking motivation, determination, and patience. Sambo is not only about executing the moves but also about gaining complete control over each skill and every move your body makes.

The Goals and Characteristics of Russian Sambo

The goals of Russian Sambo depend on the style, which is discussed later. However, the ultimate goal behind this combating style is to end a fight quickly and efficiently. It is typically done by taking the adversary to the ground, and the wrestler proceeds to execute a submission hold quickly. The practitioner usually follows the takedown with fast strikes in combat-oriented Sambo styles.

Anyone who practices Sambo must know three specific characteristics; leg locks, a seamless combination of Judo and other wrestling maneuvers, and fundamental control abilities. The employed style of Sambo also adds a few things to the basic mix. For instance, in combat-oriented Sambo, the practitioner must acquire great striking skills. Even so, Sambo is essentially an art of masterful grappling. Submissions and takedowns are its primary areas of focus.

The History of Sambo

The Origins

Sambo was developed to serve as a combination of all or the majority of the different martial arts. The main goal was to develop a style and system that offered the most efficiency. Russia, the metaphorical bridge connecting Asian and European countries, was the hubbub of various fighting styles and techniques.

Martial arts developed in either continent were quickly introduced to the Russians as they were in near direct contact with the Vikings, Mongols, Japanese, Tartar, and several other battles and fight-savvy civilizations. The styles and techniques these people donated to the Russians served as raw material for the foundation of what we now know as Russian Sambo.

Russia's elite Red Army Karate and Judo instructor, Vasili Oshchepkov, was one of the pioneers of Sambo. Like every other trainer's goal or dream, he wanted his apprentices to be the best, most skilled, and most competent in all combat systems and martial arts techniques.

Oshchepkov was among the few non-Japanese holders of a 2nd Dan black belt in Judo from Jigoro Kano. This accomplishment convinced him that he could develop a better martial arts style. He combined the moves and skills he thought were most efficient from Judo with those from Karate and several Russian native wrestling techniques.

During that time, Victor Spiridonov, a highly experienced man in Greco-Roman wrestling and other styles, worked on sorting and picking all the techniques from hand-to-hand fighting methods and leaving out what didn't work. Spiridonov was formerly injured by a bayonet during the Russo-Japanese War. This injury left his left arm lame, which undoubtedly affected his work.

Due to his injury, the style that Spiridonov employed was naturally a lot softer in retrospect. His injury made him think from an alternate, rather unusual perspective. Typically, practitioners aim to use power and strength in combat. However, Spiridonov hoped to develop an effective style that allowed him to use the opponent's strength against them. This technique would work if the practitioner deflected the adversary's aggression or power in a way they would not anticipate easily. His technique was invaluable to injured or weaker practitioners, allowing them to fight equally well. His style was officially known as "Samoz."

General Military Training, or Vseobuch, was developed in 1918 by Vladimir Lenin. This program aimed to train the Red Army under K. Voroshilov's leadership. NKVD physical training center, Dinamo, was created by Voroshilov. Several experienced and professional instructors were brought together to ensure success in this center. Spiridonov was among the first instructors who taught self-defense and wrestling techniques at Dinamo.

1923 was the year when the magic happened. Spiridonov and Oschepkov worked alongside each other to expand on and enhance the Red Army's weaponless fighting and combat system. I.V. Vasiliev and Anatoly Kharlampiev, who were exceptionally well-versed in global martial arts, also participated in this significant collaboration.

One decade later, an outline or general draft for what the world now knows as Sambo was finally ready. This outline combined all the techniques and styles that each thought to be highly efficient and effective.

Although they all worked diligently on the project, Kharlampiev is famously known as the Father of Sambo, perhaps due to his strong political connections. It's also an homage to his ability and perseverance to stay true to the martial art's formulation throughout its early initiation and developmental stages.

Additionally, Kharlampiev was the person behind the campaign for Sambo to serve as the official Soviet Union's combat sport. His campaigning dreams and efforts came to life in 1938. However, it is worth mentioning that evidence points toward Spiridonov as the first one to use the name "Sambo" in reference to the newly developed combat system.

Sambo was finally taught and employed by the Soviet military and police, and other organizations as soon as its techniques were refined and properly cataloged. However, keep in mind that the techniques underwent minor enhancements depending on the targeted or assumed group.

Sambo in the USA

It wasn't until the 1960s that Sambo started spreading outside of Russia. It appeared in other parts of the world when several practitioners of the fighting style took part in international Judo competitions. In 1968, FILA ("Fédération Internationale des Luttes Associées"), or the International Federation of Associated Wrestling Styles, recognized Judo, Sambo, and Greco-Roman wrestling as international wrestling styles.

Boris Timoshin – a Russian-born politician and a Czechoslovakian refugee – traveled to the United States in 1968. He was a Sambo practitioner and champion in college and aimed to keep training while seeking a career in Sambo instruction. Upon his arrival, he was turned down by every martial arts center he went to. Despite all the rejection, he found a place to train and teach Sambo on 23rd Street at the YMCA in New York City and formed wonderful friendships along the way.

While his Sambo teaching career only lasted until 1971, he left an incredible mark, making him one of the most legendary figures in the Sambo community. He earned the title "America's first Sambo coach" since he was the USA's first Sambo instructor.

It was during the mid-1980s that Sambo competitions gained popularity. The sport received its own organization, FIAS or International Sambo Federation, in 1985. However, the combating style's true recognition and popularity took off when Oleg Taktarov, a holder of a Russian black belt in Judo and a Sambo competitor, won the UFC 6 in 1995. Only then did an exceptional number of UFC fighters add Sambo techniques to their moves and skillsets.

Today, there are two large American Sambo organizations, the AASF or All-American SAMBO Federation and the USA Sambo.

Sambo: Is It An Olympic Sport?

In 1980, the Summer Olympics' opening ceremony in Moscow featured a youth Sambo demonstration. Despite the talk revolving around the International Olympic Committee recognizing Sambo as an official Olympic sport in 1981, the combat style is yet to become one. However, the pressure and hope persist, considering that President Vladimir Putin, an honorary FIAT president, shows ongoing support for the sport and the Sambo community's heartfelt efforts.

Modern-Day Sambo

According to the International Sambo Federation, the World Sambo Championships in Sofia, Bulgaria, in 2016 housed over 500 athletes. These participants came from 80 different countries. The exact number of people globally practicing Sambo cannot be estimated. However, in 2013 there were over 410,000 individuals practicing Sambo in Russia alone.

Sambo has a very admirable philosophy, like any martial art. This conviction promotes principles of respect, self-discipline, personal growth and development, and friendship. These values are taught to all Sambo practitioners regardless of age, race, beliefs, geographic location, or nationality, not to mention the sport's great influence on endurance, stamina, and strength. These make Sambo the perfect sport and self-defense technique for children and adults.

Subtypes of Sambo

Various Sambo styles exist. While the definitive principles of Sambo remain more or less the same, numerous variations of this sport have emerged since its first formulation. Despite the countless styles, the combat style can be broken down into Sport Sambo and Combat Sambo. In addition to these two main categories or subtypes, only four more are widely recognized by the public.

1. Sport Sambo

Sport Sambo is mainly a competitive form of Sambo and is generally similar to Judo and wrestling. For instance, a competitor must rely heavily on grappling, takedown defenses, and takedowns to win the match. Leg locks, in all their forms, are also allowed within the rules of the competition. Leg locks are very similar to armbars. However, as you can deduce from the name, they are carried out by the legs.

The current World Championship weight categories for men are 52 kg, 57kg, 62kg, 68kg, 74kg, 82kg, 90kg, 100kg, and over 100kg. For women, the weight categories are 48kg, 52kg, 56kg, 60kg, 64kg, 68kg, 72kg, 80kg, and over 80kg.

2. Combat Sambo

Combat Sambo was created solely for military use. Although Sambo stands for self-defense without weapons, Combat Sambo includes disarming techniques and weaponry. In addition to the basic Sambo moves, Combat Sambo requires executing excess grappling and striking.

Despite being created exclusively for the Russian military, Combat Sambo is now among the common competitive Sambo styles. It differs from Sport Sambo because it includes head butting, elbow and knee usage, grappling, groin strikes, punches, and kicks. It is similar to modern-day MMA. Competitors must wear shin and head guards and hand protectors in addition to the regular Sambo gear.

Combat Sambo is practiced by men only. The current World Championship weight categories are 52kg, 57kg, 62kg, 68kg, 74kg, 82kg, 90kg, 100kg, and over 100kg.

3. Freestyle Sambo

In 2004, the American Sambo Association developed the Freestyle Sambo subtype. It was an attempt to have non-Sambo practitioners participate in Sambo events, especially those who took part in Judo and Jujitsu. These events allowed several submissions typically not allowed in Sport Sambo, the chokehold executions.

4. Self-Defense Sambo

Self-defense Sambo is all about - you guessed it - defense tactics and techniques. The great thing about this Sambo subtype is it teaches practitioners to defend themselves against weapons and other attacks. The main strategy is to use the opponent's or attacker's power and aggression against them. As you recall, this was Spiridonov's main aim. His influence, alongside the spirit of Aikido and Jujitsu, is eminent in self-defense Sambo.

5. Special Sambo

Special Sambo was created for rapid response law formations and Army Special Forces. It is merely a more specialized version or subtype of the average Sambo technique. It was refined and perfected to suit the specific unit that would use it. Special Sambo is quite similar to Combat Sambo. However, each group adds a few particular aims to the mix.

6. Beach Sambo

Beach Sambo is the unconventional version of the combatting style. As the name implies, the fight is carried out on the beach, eliminating the mat wrestling tradition. A rule that the combat's duration lasts three minutes is also employed. There are no penalties, and the time count begins as soon as the first move is assessed. The usual competition uniform is also modified. For the 2016 Asian Beach Games in Danang, Vietnam, the weight categories for men were 62kg, 74kg, 90kg, and over 90kg. For women, the weight categories were 56kg, 64kg, 72kg, and over 72kg.

Sambo quickly became an international sport due to its incorporation of numerous national martial arts. The self-defense technique has already gathered enthusiasts in over 80 countries, and the number is still growing. International tournaments and championships are held globally, meaning specialized Sambo schools or instructors are in different parts of the world.

Sambo practitioners take great pride in their sport. Instructors, trainees, and even opposing wrestlers are united by solidarity and friendship. All wrestlers must show respect to their opponents.

Chapter 2: Comparing Sambo to Judo, Jiu-Jitsu, and Wrestling

This chapter examines the similarities and differences between Sambo, Judo, Jiu-Jitsu, and Wrestling. It explains each martial art's unique style to help you decide which best suits your needs.

Core Aspect Comparison: Sambo vs. Judo vs. BJJ vs. Wrestling

The Core Aspects of Sambo

President.az, CC BY 4.0 <https://creativecommons.org/licenses/by/4.0>, via Wikimedia Commons
https://commons.wikimedia.org/wiki/File:Sambo_at_the_2015_European_Games.jpg

Sambo is a martial art originating in Russia but is recognized and practiced internationally. It is a hybrid of Judo and Wrestling, developed during the early 20th century. The primary goal of Sambo is to neutralize or disable an opponent as quickly as possible with effective joint locks, chokes, throws, kicks, punches, and other techniques. In addition to being very functional on its own merits, Sambo relies heavily on Judo throws and techniques to be effective. A Sambo practitioner must have a solid foundation in the art and excellent takedown skills to takedown opponents. In contrast, other martial arts styles focus more on stand-up techniques and less on takedowns.

The Core Aspects of Judo

Korea.net / Korean Culture and Information Service (Photographer name), CC BY-SA 2.0
<https://creativecommons.org/licenses/by-sa/2.0>, via Wikimedia Commons
https://commons.wikimedia.org/wiki/File:KOCIS_Korea_Judo_Kim_Jaebum_London_36
_(7696361164).jpg

Judo is a martial art originating in Japan but recognized internationally. It focuses more on throws, grappling, chokes, armlocks, kneebars, and kicks to the head and neck area (not groin shots) than Sambo does. Judo is one of the most effective martial arts for self-defense against bigger, stronger, or heavier opponents and has its place in MMA (Mixed Martial Arts). It is an excellent choice for those looking to compete professionally in grappling tournaments.

The Core Aspects of Jiu-Jitsu

CFS SAMBO FRANCE, CC BY-SA 2.0 <https://creativecommons.org/licenses/by-sa/2.0>, via Wikimedia Commons
https://commons.wikimedia.org/wiki/File:Grand_Prix_Paris_de_Sambo_IMG_1923_(341 52646253).jpg

Brazilian Jiu-Jitsu is a martial art with roots in Jiu-Jitsu. It is mainly about grappling and ground fighting. They do not focus on stand-up techniques like kicking and punching. It is very effective for self-defense against bigger, stronger, or heavier opponents because they will most likely take the fight to the ground where your smaller stature won't matter as much. However, BJJ can be more dangerous than other martial arts styles because of its focus on grappling and ground fighting. If you are not trained properly, your opponent will use their superior size and strength against you and endanger your safety.

The Core Aspects of Wrestling

https://commons.wikimedia.org/wiki/File:0432-SahinThrowsWood.jpg

Wrestling is the oldest grappling sport, with origins dating back as far as ancient Greece (even further if we consider its common roots with hunting). In self-defense, wrestling is one of the most effective martial arts because it protects you from larger and stronger opponents by taking them down quickly. Considering an opponent's size and strength while fighting on your feet also makes wrestling a very practical grappling form for MMA, which is now one of the most popular sports worldwide.

Differences in Origins

Sambo was developed in Russia during the early 20th century. It combines Judo and Wrestling, making it very effective for self-defense purposes (especially against larger, stronger opponents) and limiting its practicality to grappling situations like MMA.

Judo originated in Japan and was introduced in 1882 by Kano Jigoro Shihan. Judo is an educational method derived from martial arts, focusing on throws, grappling, chokes, armlocks, kneebars, kicks to the head and neck area (not groin shots), etc. It is very effective for self-defense against larger and stronger opponents, but it can be dangerous if trained improperly because of its focus on ground fighting. It became an Olympic sport in 1964.

Brazilian Jiu-Jitsu is derived from Jiu-Jitsu but focuses primarily on grappling and ground fighting rather than stand-up techniques like punching and kicking. The Japanese taught their art to Brazilians. An expert Judoka, Mitsuyo Maeda, went to Sao Paulo and taught the Brazilian people his art.

Wrestling is a very old sport that started in the Sumerian era – 5000 years ago. It is one of the most practical grappling martial arts because it protects you from larger and stronger opponents by allowing you to take them down quickly.

Differences in Goals/Aims

Although Sambo was derived from Judo and has many similarities with other martial arts, it differs greatly in philosophy. Judo teaches mental calmness and focuses on avoiding conflict, which aligns with the philosophy of all Japanese martial art forms.

On the other hand, Sambo allows you to fight for victory by all means necessary, even if that means striking your opponent. It is especially true for Combat Sambo, where techniques like kicks are allowed. Conversely, Sport Sambo has a calmer approach similar to Judo.

Brazilian Jiu Jitsu's philosophy is that any smaller or weaker person can successfully defend themselves against a larger opponent. It allows them to apply, most notably joint locks, to defeat the other person. One of the main objectives of Brazilian Jiu-Jitsu is to lock and immobilize by using your hands and legs.

Finally, Wrestling idealizes the idea of control over the opponent rather than attacking them. Wrestling is about gaining a superior body position to pin your opponent onto their back and getting out of that position by performing a technique or executing an escape maneuver before you are pinned.

Differences in Technique

Sambo focuses on techniques for leg locks, throwing, groundwork, and submissions. Sport Sambo does not allow chokeholds in competition and has a few restrictions on specific gripping and holding techniques.

On the other hand, Combat Sambo was developed for the military and closely resembles Mixed Martial Arts. This Sambo variant allows MMA forms of striking and grappling and more combative punching, elbow and knee kicks, soccer kicks, chokeholds, and headbutts.

The distinction between Sambo and Brazilian jiu-jitsu (BJJ) is that Combat Sambo rules and regulations do not allow ground fighting without throws or other combative tactics, as opposed to BJJ's allowance of these maneuvers.

The objective of Brazilian jiu-jitsu is to force an adversary to the ground to neutralize possible physical or size advantages through ground fighting methods, chokeholds, and joint locks.

Judo and Sambo have very similar fighting styles. Both arts use a wide range of throws and grappling to take an opponent down. However, as discussed, Combat Sambo allows additional strikes and knee and elbow kicks that are not allowed in Judo competitions or training.

Wrestling rules allow opponents to continue fighting on their feet after gaining control over one another - known as "top position" or "top control." The objective of wrestling is to pin your opponent on his back for long enough to win the match by reaching an agreed-upon number of points.

Differences in Rules

The governing ruleset of any martial art usually addresses three major criteria:

1. Techniques allowed – for example, some martial arts allow chokeholds and strikes while others don't.

2. Winning Criteria - when can a competitor be declared a winner? It can be scoring the maximum points, having a specific point lead, or executing the perfect maneuver.

3. Foul or illegal moves and the penalties imposed.

4. A detailed point system awarding a specific number of points for specific moves (or deducting points for illegal moves)

Rules of Sambo and Combat Sambo

There are four ways to win a match in Combat Sambo:

1. Throw an opponent to the ground while standing. How you throw your opponent must show control and intent, i.e., perform a perfect throw while remaining in a standing position.

2. Get an 8-point lead over your opponent.

3. In a submission, the referee stops the match when the opponent becomes unconscious or taps out of fear (achieved by locking the opponent).

4. A competitor has gained more points than the opponent at the end of the match. This is achieved by performing throws, takedowns, and holds, leading to your victory.

Throws and Pins are scored for Combat Sambo.

If the opponent is pinned for 10 to 19 seconds, 2 points are awarded. If the opponent is pinned for more than 20 seconds, 4 points are awarded.

Throws are scored depending on your position during and after the throw and how the opponent falls. More points are given when you are upright during and after the throw.

Illegal techniques and stalling are penalized in a competition.

Rules of Judo

Judo's rules are identical to Sambo's because the objective is to throw, takedown, or immobilize an opponent onto their back. An ideal score or Ippon is awarded when you have an opponent pinned onto their back for 20 seconds. An Ippon immediately ends the match.

In Judo, all submissions are allowed except those resulting in a broken bone or joint lock on the elbow and fingers. In addition, there is no "scoring" position during competition other than gaining control of your opponent's body through pins or holds. Any amount of time with your opponent on their back is considered a legal pin.

A Waza-ari (or half a point) is awarded for less ideal throws or when the opponent is pinned down for a shorter duration than required to score an Ippon. Scoring two waza-aris in a match is an Ippon and immediately ends the match.

Finally, a yuko is the smallest score for less effective techniques.

The aim is to score a perfect Ippon to overtake the opponent and win the match with maximum points.

Rules of Jiu-Jitsu

Jiu-Jitsu matches are usually 3 to 5 minutes, depending on the category. Competitors are awarded 2, 3, or 4 points for achieving dominant positions or executing techniques. A victory is gained by the opponent with the most points or on successful submission.

Rules of Wrestling

Wrestling matches are broken down into two rounds, each lasting three minutes. Competitors get points by:

- **Takedown** - A competitor gets their opponent onto the ground with at least one foot on the floor between them and the edge of the ring or on the ground.

- **Escape** – A competitor gets away from their opponent's control and back to a standing position with at least one foot not touching the floor within the ring (or lines) without being controlled by an opponent.

- **Reversal** - A competitor is on the ground, and their opponent has full control of them; they can get points if they reverse the hold so that they have full control.

- **Penalties** - Competitors can get negative points for illegal holds or technical violations.

Differences in Uniform

These martial arts demand quick footwork, and techniques revolve around complex body movements. The uniforms for each sport are designed to allow maximum flexibility and movement. Sambo, Judo, and BJJ have very similar attire, with minor differences. However, wrestling has a unique uniform, quite different from the others.

Sambo uniforms consist of four pieces; the jacket, pants, shoes, and belt. The uniform is red or blue, and the jacket is often reversible. The uniform is called a Kurtka.

Judo's uniform usually only includes a judogi (similar to a karate gi). Judogi is usually white and comprises three parts, jacket, pants, and belt. It should fit similarly to Sambo or Jiu-jitsu uniforms without being too loose or tight on the body.

Jiu-jitsu's uniform includes a Gi similar to Judo, a jacket, pants, and a belt. It can be any color, but white is most common for competitions. It comes with a belt ranking system from white to black depending on the time you have trained and your rank within the school or association.

Wrestling uniforms are specific to the competition held. In college, folk style is the most common, with a singlet or tight shorts and shirt worn without shoes during practices. Freestyle competitions wear tighter uniforms and wrestling boots for footwear. Women's folk style wear spandex-like short suits instead of singlets to minimize the risk of skin infections from mats.

Belt System Comparison

Sambo, Jiu-Jitsu, and Judo have their own belt systems. These indicate the rank of a competitor within their sport. More often than not, expertise is also measured based on performance at a regional and global level. Similar to other sports, martial arts rank their practitioners at a global level. However, to feature in this ranking system, a practitioner must participate and compete against the world's best.

In Sambo, there are seven ranks. Each rank is held for one year, starting with Rookie or level 1 (white belt) to 7th year, 2nd Master (yellow, orange, green, blue, brown, and finally black). Various organizations issue the title of "master of sport" or "international master of sport" to those who excel nationally and internationally.

Brazilian Jiu-Jitsu belts are divided by color, ranked from white to red, and consist of eight belts. A minimum number of hours of training is required for each belt level before being tested; usually, the higher the rank, the more hours are required to achieve that next belt or title.

Judo also has a belt system progression, with black belts being the highest.

Wrestling does not have a defined belt system for competitors. Still, it does have a progression level based on practice. The world ranking is based on performance in competitions.

Cross-Training Opportunities

Many athletes compete in more than one sport and experience success due to their similarities. Sambo, BJJ, and Judo are very similar, offering cross-training opportunities. Wrestling is a form of submission grappling, and Sambo is heavily influenced by Judo. Wrestling uses similar submissions to BJJ, making it easier for those who do both to transition seamlessly from one art to the other.

Each sport has different rules. Still, they all work on similar concepts, movements, and techniques involving takedowns, submissions, and using the legs. The similarities between these arts make it easy for those training in one art to cross-train with another similar art increasing their success rates within each sport and making them more knowledgeable practitioners overall.

For example, a Combat Sambo-trained athlete will do very well in MMA competitions, thanks to cross-training in Judo (throws and grappling) and strikes, elbow, and knee kicks from Combat Sambo training. Due to these skills, Sambo fighters are rightly called the most ferocious of the lot.

Competitions

Dedicated training in martial arts usually culminates in a competitive mindset. All four art forms have developed over the years and have seen a significant rise in professional world competitions and local or regional events.

Sambo competitions are governed by FIAS (International Sambo Federation), the international governing body. Many events are held yearly, with medals awarded to winners based on their rank and belt system levels. The most noteworthy events are the World Cup and other World Championships. The Sambo Federation has recently acquired recognition from the IOC (International Olympic Committee), and it could soon become an Olympic sport.

Judo competitions usually have many athletes competing at major tournaments, such as the Olympic Games, world championships, or regional meets. In addition, smaller invitationals around the country offer chances for athletes to compete in their respective divisions.

Brazilian Jiu-jitsu is governed by the IBJJF (International Brazilian Jiu-Jitsu Federation), which organizes tournaments and championships. Many competitions are held worldwide for all belt levels, for men and women.

Wrestling is one of the most popular sports and also an Olympics sport. It is governed by FILA (International Federation of Associated Wrestling Styles), which organizes various meets and competitions.

Benefits of Sambo Compared to the Other Martial Arts

Sambo is a great opportunity for those interested in martial arts but has no idea where to begin. So, Sambo has many benefits making it a great choice for beginners.

Sambo is an effective martial art that offers fitness training by employing cardiovascular exercise, strength conditioning, and self-defense skills.

Those interested in learning Sambo can take classes with other students at their skill level, making new friends sharing the same interests. This interaction builds camaraderie and is a great way to meet others with similar goals.

Sambo offers many opportunities for those wanting to compete, increasing self-confidence and providing a great outlet for stress relief, often missing in other sports or activities. It encourages discipline, high physical fitness standards, mental strength, and perseverance.

Sambo can be practiced by anyone, regardless of age or fitness level; it is an excellent option for children because it teaches discipline without being overly aggressive. It also helps build self-esteem while increasing coordination skills that could improve academic performance at school.

The belt system in Sambo acts as a guide for students on their progress. The seniority of belts reflects a person's knowledge level.

The Most Effective Martial Art

Although in principle, all martial arts have their pros and cons in technique, a Sambo-trained individual will win in a fight. Sambo training, especially Combat Sambo, is hardcore and involves striking, grappling, kicks, and weapon-disarming techniques. It is the best martial art for self-defense and a great form of fitness training with plenty of mental and physical benefits.

Sambo differs from other martial arts because it utilizes takedowns using all parts of the body, including legs and head, making Sambo stand out among others. Judo is the mother of Sambo and BJJ, albeit with certain restrictions and less brutality.

On the other hand, wrestling teaches a trainee to manipulate the opponent's strength and use it against them. It is a sport where practitioners can apply their skills in real-life situations, making wrestling a great choice for self-defense and recreational activity.

To summarize, Sambo is a fantastic martial art and self-defense system that can be practiced by almost anyone, regardless of age or fitness level. It offers many physical and mental benefits, so it is an excellent choice for those interested in learning effective fighting techniques and seeking general health improvements.

Availability of Training Facilities and Trainers

Sambo is available at various locations across the country, including military bases and colleges. Perhaps not as many as Judo. However, visit online resources or contact the federation to determine a training center near you. As far as trainers are concerned, many experienced martial artists offer lessons in different hand-to-hand combat styles, including Sambo.

Judo is a sport practiced by millions of people around the world. Many are drawn to this martial art because it focuses on grappling techniques, which can be used in real-life situations more often than striking moves. Judo is taught at most gyms and fitness centers across the country, making it an ideal choice for those wanting to train regularly and in an organized discipline.

Jiu-jitsu is considered one of the most effective martial arts in ground fighting – with elements similar to Sambo, Judo, and Wrestling. Jiu-Jitsu has become increasingly popular across the world and can be practiced by anyone. Many Jiu-Jitsu training centers are across the country where practitioners can take classes, usually alongside a fitness program.

Wrestling is a combat sport involving grappling techniques and offers physical and mental benefits. So, it is an excellent choice for self-defense and recreational activity. Wrestling training facilities are commonly available at gyms and fitness centers nationwide.

All the martial arts described in this chapter have their philosophies, origins, techniques, rules, competitive advantages, and benefits. However, in some form, nearly all the art forms have been derived from Judo.

Choose the discipline based on the availability of training facilities and trainers and your physical capability.

If you aim to only practice for self-defense, any martial art will be helpful. If you want to compete internationally, go for Judo or wrestling, as it is easy to find qualified masters near you. Brazilian Jiu-Jitsu is a great choice for those interested in ground fighting, while Sambo offers an effective blend of technique and combat.

Chapter 3: Before Starting: Sambo Essentials and Benefits

If you're reading this book, you've decided Sambo is the martial art for you. Or perhaps your child has already taken to it, and now you want to know more about their chosen sport. Either way, read on. Chapter 3 gives you all the information before starting Sambo, including gear and uniform requirements, benefits of learning this particular martial art, why it's worth learning, and much more.

Types of Sambo

Sambo can be categorized into three types based on the techniques - Sports Sambo, Combat Sambo, or Freestyle Sambo.

1. Sports Sambo

Sports Sambo combines Judo and Wrestling - allowing techniques like leg locks and takedowns with a focus on throws. Sport Sambo does not allow chokeholds.

2. Freestyle Sambo

Freestyle Sambo is a more independent version of the sport allowing all techniques, including submission, striking, and grappling. This form focuses on throws, takedowns, and locks.

Freestyle Sambo was introduced by The American Sambo Association. Freestyle Sambo allows any grappling technique, including those not allowed in Sport or Combat styles. Techniques like neck cranks and twisted leg holds are allowed to gain submissions. Striking is not allowed. Mastering throws is key to winning the match.

3. Combat Sambo

Combat Sambo is a more realistic version of the sport, including striking and grappling, making it closer to Mixed Martial Arts.

Combat Sambo combines Judo, Wrestling, and Jiu-Jitsu, allowing techniques like grappling, striking, chokeholds, and leg locks. It also allows techniques of elbow and knee kicks, groin strikes, and headbutts. It is the most aggressive form of Sambo.

11 Compelling Reasons to Learn Sambo

1. Sambo Is a Superior Martial Art

Sambo was derived from Judo in the Soviet Union as a combat form for the military. This positions Sambo as a unique martial art - having the age-old grappling techniques of Judo and superior Mixed Martial Arts combat skills. A Sambo Master is skilled in grappling, takedowns, dominating, and on-ground submissions. Therefore, a Sambo Master is almost unbeatable in any combat situation.

2. Sambo Is a Perfect Self-Defense System for Everyone, Young and Old

Anyone can learn Sambo. It doesn't matter if you're old or young, big and tall, or small and quick because Sambo works well with every body type. This martial art will teach you to defend yourself while also teaching respect and discipline. The locks, holds, and groundwork learned in Sambo prepare you for any threatening situation.

3. Sambo Is a Competitive Sport

Many think Sambo only works as a self-defense system, but it is also competitive. You don't have to compete if you don't want to. But there are many competitions for those who do. It's fun and exciting and helps your fitness level improve quickly. Recently, the IOC recognized the sport of Sambo, and it might soon become an Olympic sport.

4. Physical Fitness and Endurance

Sambo is an excellent workout for the body. It trains every muscle, leading to increased strength and endurance. Since Sambo involves so many rapid movements, it's a great cardio workout, too. Whether you want to get in shape fast or give yourself a full-body workout that'll leave you feeling amazing when it's over, Sambo is the way to go.

5. Sambo's Success in MMA

Sambo is a Mixed Martial Art. Sambo practitioners are trained in grappling and striking styles, allowing them to excel at ground combat and stand-up fighting. Sambo fighters are known to be the best at all MMA techniques - grappling, throwing, and takedowns. Sambo Masters are also very good at submissions and reversals. They are known as the most ferocious fighters in the sport.

6. Sambo Teaches Discipline and Respect

Sambo is a discipline and respect-based art. It teaches students to be aware of their actions on the mat and in life. Sambo practitioners are expected to show self-discipline at all times, not only while training. Sambo teaches students to be humble and respectful towards themselves and others.

7. Physical Strength and Dexterity

Sambo demands much from the body - flexibility, coordination skills, stamina, and endurance; it's an all-around workout for your entire body. You'll get in shape fast and develop unbelievable strength with Sambo training. Whether you want to get stronger or more flexible, Sambo will help you achieve your goals.

8. Sambo Is a Valuable Skill for Law Enforcement and the Military

Law enforcement officers and military personnel are often called upon to subdue aggressive people who could be armed with weapons. More often than not, this requires grappling skills. Sambo is a very useful tool in these professions as it prepares people to take on dangerous situations.

9. Mental Strength and Wellness

Sambo offers a great workout for the body and an excellent way to soothe frazzled nerves. The concentration and energy you'll gain from training in this martial art will also help keep your mind sharp. Physical activity has been proven to lower stress levels, making Sambo perfect for those who are always on the go or constantly dealing with stressful situations.

10. Learn to Prevent Injury

Sambo training is great for preventing injuries. At its core, Sambo is Self Defense. Sambo will effectively help defend against aggression and teach you to prevent injury while taking a fall. Those training in Sambo learns to protect themselves against injury, which can be helpful for those with jobs or lifestyles in dangerous situations.

11. Sambo Provides an Excellent Base for Other Martial Arts

Anyone interested in joining other martial arts skills would benefit from starting with Sambo. The groundwork learned as part of this particular martial art is very beneficial when adding other martial arts to your collection. In the previous chapter, we learned that Sambo is very similar to Brazilian Jiu-Jitsu (BJJ), Wrestling, and Judo. Due to this, many people begin training in Sambo before moving on to BJJ or Judo, as these arts are more popular than Sambo among the general public. However, you can't beat a good solid foundation.

Sambo Gear and Equipment

You'll need certain equipment and gear to get the most from your Sambo training. Sambo gear is very similar to MMA gear, mainly consisting of the Sambovka, Helmet, Guards, Gloves, and Mouth Shields.

The Sambovka

The Sambovka is a traditional vest worn by Sambists when training. It is designed to be tightly form-fitting and provides ample protection without compromising agility or movement. This jacket is usually red or blue and worn with a belt and shorts to match. A competitor is usually required to have both blue and red-colored sets so they can be visually distinguished on the mat.

Sambovka does not portray the rank or expertise of the competitor in any way - there is no identification of rank on the uniform.

The Sambovka has strict specifications for material and design. It uses a specific fabric variant with robust seams and wings on the shoulders. A belt is worn around the Sambovka to secure it during a match. Additionally, the sleeve should be no more than 10 cm in width and reach the wrist exactly. The jacket's flaps should be only about 15 cm below the uniform's belt.

Helmet

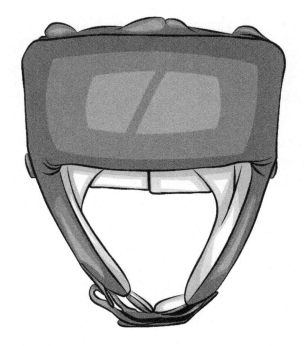

The Sambo helmet is like the boxing helmet and is worn to protect the competitor's head. It should be very lightweight so as not to hinder movement or cause discomfort during training sessions.

It is made from firm but soft plastic and has visors in front for proper visibility when sparring with competitors on all sides. Additionally, it provides protection from accidental knee or elbow strikes. The helmet has straps on the chin and back of the head to protect from accidental injuries.

Gloves

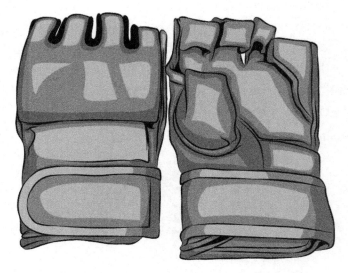

Sambo gloves are very similar to boxing and MMA gloves. They provide all-around protection for the hands, wrists, fingers, and knuckles during training sessions with competitors. The glove also helps secure a firm grip when grappling or fighting in matches while protecting you from accidental injury.

The Sambist should always have red and blue gloves.

Mouth Guards

The mouth guard is considered a vital piece of equipment in Sambo as it helps prevent chipping or broken teeth when taking falls. However, many people don't wear them because they can be uncomfortable and affect breathing during training sessions.

Groin Guard

Groin guards are not mandatory in Sambo but are highly recommended. They help prevent injuries to the groin during training sessions with competitors on all sides.

Shoes

Shoe specifications are not strict in Sambo. Ideally, you should wear wrestling shoes or boxing boots with a good grip for traction on the mat. These shoes should have a snug fit and adequately support the ankle and heels. Sambo shoes should not be fancy and have any parts sticking out, which could cause injuries.

Shorts

Sambo shorts must be the same color as the jacket. These should be about 2/3s the length of your thigh, reaching about 2.5 inches above your knee. Shorts with pockets are not allowed. The color of the shorts must match the jacket.

What to Wear to Training

You don't need any particular clothes or gear to train in, but you should wear something comfortable that allows your body a full range of motion.

Judogi is the most common uniform worn for Sambo training – it's required at higher levels (national and international competitions). A judogi consists of a jacket, belt, and pants. Some practitioners wear a Sambovka instead of the judogi when training with other Sambists.

You should wear socks but no shoes or slippers to training sessions as they can cause injuries during grappling and throwing.

Discuss the uniform with your trainer. Inform him about any financial constraints to purchasing appropriate gear, as many masters will donate or suggest alternate training attire.

What to Expect Before You Consider Training for Sambo

Consider the following before you decide to start Sambo training:

- Sparring and competition include a lot of throwing, takedowns, grappling, tackling, and lifting your opponent to slam them down or toss them across the mat. You might want to start with Judo if you're not prepared for such physical contact during training. Make sure you're in good health before you start.

- You need to have a calm mind or be able to control your emotions; otherwise, training can get very frustrating. New techniques are always being taught, so it's important to learn them quickly and don't let yourself become upset if someone beats you on the mat. Just keep trying until you get it right.

- You need to follow instructions and listen carefully. Otherwise, you won't learn what you should. Practice concentration during class – it'll come in handy later on.

- You need to be a self-starter. If you can't motivate yourself and work hard without being told, then Sambo isn't the martial art for you.

- You need to handle pain. Sambo is painful. Getting thrown, taken down, or held can hurt you, but your body will get used to it over time.

- You need to work well with others. Working in a team is important; you'll learn how quickly when training.

- You need to learn quickly. No matter your age, if you have trouble learning something, ask for help from the instructors. They are there to help you.

- You need to move fast when necessary. A lot of the throws and takedowns you learn will happen fast, so you need to be able to react quickly. Otherwise, you will end up on the ground.

- Sambo training could be expensive. You need to be prepared for the costs of uniforms, sparring gear, and training fees.

- Training can take a long time. Becoming good at the sport requires persistence and dedication.

- Sparring and competition can be dangerous, so training well before entering matches is important.

- You need to be ready for disappointment. If you don't win, keep practicing. Most athletes have lost more matches than they've won.

- Depending on where you live, you might need to travel for training. Sambo is practiced worldwide, but there are not many clubs in North America – you might need to travel.

You'll probably have lots of fun. Sambo involves a ton of physical activity and is a great way to get in shape while learning something new. There's nothing better than getting a takedown and pinning your opponent.

Sambo Practice and Training

Once you have all of your gear, it's time to get started with actual Sambo practice.

Sambo is a dynamic martial art involving many different throws and grappling techniques. To start this martial art, focus first on learning the proper technique for each throw or submission hold before applying them during sparring sessions against partners.

Although there is no formal curriculum for Sambo, it's best to start by learning the basic throws and grappling techniques before moving on to more advanced ones. You need to learn a few basic principles to practice correctly so as not to injure yourself or your opponent during training sessions:

- **Grip Fighting** - when you are both trying to gain a good grip on each other to execute a proper throw or submission move.

- **Takedowns** - where one person lifts their opponent and slams them down onto the mat, bringing them down with an arm across their chest while they land hard on the ground.

- **Throws** - where both practitioners are standing, one person throws their opponent down by tripping or pushing them.

- **Ground Fighting** - Once a competitor has been thrown to the ground, the attacker will set themselves in a position for better defense, preparing an attack on their opponent after gaining control of their body.

- **Submissions** - one competitor holds their opponent in a position that puts them at risk of injury, like limbs, joints, or the neck. The defender submits to end the fight.

- **Pinning Techniques** - After gaining control of your partner's body on the ground and immobilizing it with your weight to prevent escape, you can pin them down with these techniques.

How Much Does It Cost to Become a Sambo Master?

The cost of learning Sambo will depend on where you are located and what your instructor charges per lesson.

Sambo instructors are a rare find in regions outside of Russia. Hence, this could be an expensive art to learn. Typically, similar to an MMA gym, a Sambo gym membership could cost you between $100 and $150 per month.

With Sambo, like the other martial arts, some of your fees will go towards equipment and gear you need for training sessions.

Some other factors that will determine costs are:

- **Location:** If you are located in a big city, the prices of lessons can be higher due to demand.

- **Instructor:** Some instructors will charge more than others based on their experience and reputation as an instructor or competitor.

- **Group Class vs. Private Lessons:** Group classes usually cost less per lesson, but the number of sessions required to become proficient at Sambo is more than with private lessons.

- **Size of Training Arena:** If the training area is small, equipment will need to be shared, which can affect costs.

A Typical Sambo Training Session

Observing a training session with your instructor is best to learn more about Sambo.

Typically, there will be warm-up exercises led by the instructor. These exercises are designed to increase your strength and endurance and help you with breathing control before getting into sparring or grappling with a training partner.

After the warm-ups, you will learn the basic throws and takedowns. There are many different throws to learn, each with its benefits.

Once these techniques have been mastered, you can learn more advanced throws and grappling moves.

If possible, it would be best to get at least one sparring partner with experience in Sambo so they can give you feedback on your technique and help correct mistakes.

A training session will typically involve performing techniques repetitively until you develop muscle memory. Some sessions will also be set up to test your skill with a match. Matches are usually with opponents of the same skill levels.

Levels of Sambo Mastery

Sambo training is divided into seven years; each year gets you one step closer to becoming a master. You start as a rookie in the first year, and finally, in the seventh year, a student progresses to become a master.

This chapter outlined the basics of Sambo, a unique martial art. If you are looking for an intense workout that improves your coordination and reflexes while also learning some self-defense techniques in the process, Sambo could be just what you need. After reading this guide on how to get started, you will have a better idea about all the benefits available from learning this particular martial art.

Sambo is a unique art form with a rich philosophy that suits students of all mindsets. You have a Sambo form for those who want to focus on clean throws and also a variant for those wanting more aggressive kicks and strikes.

The chapter has discussed considerations to keep in mind before starting your Sambo journey, the costs involved, equipment and other essentials, and the benefits of becoming a Sambo Student.

Chapter 4: Throwing Techniques

For the most part, Sambo is practiced as a grappling art. Grappling is generally defined as two or more athletes competing against each other to achieve a position of dominance where they can apply submissions to their opponent, render them unconscious, or otherwise defeat them. This chapter focuses on the most basic throws in Sambo. The techniques chosen in this chapter are the most beginner-friendly and effective for grappling with a resisting opponent.

The Basics of Throws

When learning these techniques, understanding the importance of wrestling or grappling, in general, is essential. Grappling is about minimizing damage while maximizing control over the opponent. The most important part of any Sambo throw is the clinch, where the grappler secures a body lock on his opponent to limit his opponent's movement. Once the grappler has established his grip, he can use throwing techniques with proper execution and control over his opponent.

There are different variations when it comes to grappling. Each aims to limit the opponent's movements and attack.

https://pixabay.com/photos/jiu-jitsu-fight-martial-arts-2184597/

Effective grapplers in Sambo use the clinch whenever possible. It gives them a great advantage in controlling their opponents by limiting their movement and increasing grappling efficiency. For this reason, many throws involve gripping the shoulder or underarm area. However, other grips like waist-locks and hip-locks are also common.

Starting with a clinch gives you the advantage and opportunity to grapple.

https://www.pxfuel.com/en/free-photo-jdshl

From this point, the grappler can execute his throw by placing his foot or leg behind one of his opponent's feet and pushing him off balance. This should be done immediately after gripping the opponent so he has no time to react before being thrown. The most important part of executing a technique is to push your opponent off balance, not lift them. Lifting your opponent can lead to many problems during the throw, such as floating or stalling in the air with no control over your opponent's body. Once you push them off balance and establish superior positioning on top of their body, it is easy to finish the technique by locking a submission hold or executing an elbow or strike on your opponent.

These Sambo throws are very effective in combat sports like MMA and self-defense because they attack the opponent's whole body and require little energy from the grappler, who has already established superior positioning over his opponent. Grappling is more efficient than striking, but it is harder to learn and execute effectively. These throws can be practiced as a warm-up or as a drill at the end of grappling training before transitioning to effective submission holds or strikes.

Understand the importance of proper positioning before attempting these techniques. Against a resisting opponent, it is imperative to use a superior position to gain control over their body so they cannot escape. Proper positioning is key to success when applying submissions or strikes to your opponent after a throw.

Remember, Sambo throws are based on pushing the opponent off balance rather than lifting them. Pushing them off balance gives you more control over his body and makes it harder for your opponent to resist as you transition into an effective strike or submission hold.

Do not try to lift your opponent during these techniques; it gives them a chance to stall and resist, putting you in a worse position than when you started. Attempting a throw with improper positioning is like punching someone while standing on one leg. You cannot generate the force necessary to do it effectively, and you will likely fall over while attempting to execute the technique.

Always look for the clinch when starting a grappling exchange with an opponent. Grappling is more efficient than striking in most cases, but it requires proper positioning before any technique can be applied successfully. Attempting a throw without controlling your opponent's body will lead to losing your positioning and neither of you gaining any advantage.

Training for these throws can be done after grappling exchanges or as a warm-up before transitioning into submission holds or strikes. The throws are meant to be executed quickly, so your muscles must be loose before attempting them.

Basic Sambo Throwing Techniques

1. Takedown

The single most important wrestling technique is the takedown. No grappling exchanges can be won in combat sports without the ability to execute a successful throw. Even when striking techniques are applied, throwing a grappler and establishing a top position on the ground is much easier and more effective.

Executing a Takedown: To execute a simple outside leg trip, you must first establish a good grip on your opponent. Once you have a stronghold over them, block the hips and push the outside leg back with your inside leg. You aim to send your opponent tumbling forward with his legs outstretched as he falls. Follow through by dropping down on top of them and securing a mounted position.

Takedown

If your opponent turns or twists while you attempt this move, follow through and throw him to the ground anyway. It is not as efficient as the proper technique, but you will still be in a better position.

2. Judo Sweep

The basic Judo sweep involves establishing a double underhook grip on your opponent and thrusting your hips back as you pull forward with your shoulders. If executed correctly, this move should send your opponent tumbling over you and crashing to the ground.

Judo Sweep

Attempting a Judo sweep without proper control over your opponent will result in you being thrown and placed on your back. So, establish the underhook grip before attempting this technique.

3. Back Toss

A basic Sambo back toss is executed by grabbing one of your opponent's arms, jumping up, and simultaneously pulling down on their shoulder with your arm. This move leads directly into a mounted position, making it efficient to take control of the fight from your opponent.

A back toss requires proper timing and positioning to be effective, so you need complete control over your opponent before attempting this technique. If you get thrown during the process, you will not be able to follow through and mount your opponent.

4. Knee Pick

The knee pick is the simplest of all Sambo throws. Hook your foot behind one of the opponent's knees and lift, forcing them over onto their back with you on top of them. This technique can only be used when both fighters face each other, so it is not as useful in MMA competitions as other throws.

Knee Pick

Grabbing both legs and pulling with your arms will give you more leverage than attempting to pick up only one leg. However, this move is still quite easy to execute without proper positioning or strength.

5. Back Drop

This technique is very similar to a Judo throw; the difference is that you must plant your feet against the ground before lifting your opponent. Take a wide stance, and bend down low while gripping both of their arms tightly with your head up. This move can be blocked or easily countered if you are not in the proper position, so it should be used as a surprise tactic instead of an ordinary throw.

Back Drop

Once you have pulled your opponent off balance, follow through by throwing them back onto the ground. If their legs are not completely outstretched, you might be forced backward instead of forward. The goal is to slam them down underneath you for a mounted position.

6. Arm Drag

A Sambo arm drag is like a professional wrestling move. You must grip both of your opponent's arms and pull them in one direction while pushing your legs against their legs. Like the knee pick, an arm drag only works when facing each other square-on instead of side-by-side.

An effective arm drag can be difficult to execute without proper control and positioning, but it is an incredibly powerful move. Since the Sambo practitioner is not on top of his opponent during this technique, he can easily transition into another throw or submission hold.

7. Leg Trip

This move requires minimal technical skill, making it an excellent move for beginners. Sweep your foot under one of your opponent's feet and pull it toward your body while pushing against their upper body with both hands. By utilizing this simple technique, you will swiftly bring them down to the ground.

An effective leg trip can be blocked or countered by an opponent who is ready for it, so this technique should be used at close range or as a surprise tactic. A leg trip is usually followed by additional grappling techniques like a clinch throw or half-guard throw that act as follow-ups to the initial throw.

8. Shoulder Roll

The shoulder roll is an advanced technique most effective when combined with other throws and takedowns. Grip your opponent's neck and shoulders, twist and pull in one direction while pushing forward with your hips. The goal is to quickly move from a standing position into a mount or side-mount position once the throw has been executed successfully.

Shoulder Roll

The initial grip must be incredibly tight to prevent the opponent from countering the move. The proper angle and rotation must occur to pull into a mount or side-mount position, so this technique is difficult for beginners.

9. Sprawl

The sprawl is a counter-throwing technique only used when escaping an opponent's takedown. Push your hips back, bend down low, and quickly kick your feet into your opponent's stomach, causing them to fly over you as you drop down to the ground below them.

This technique must be executed quickly for the best chance of success. So, it is best used when your opponent is holding you too close or attempting to knee your stomach. If they complete their takedown, you can fall back into a side-mount position on top of them.

The sprawl is also a defensive technique to prevent yourself from being taken down. It is an important technique used offensively or defensively during Sambo competitions and practice sessions.

10. Throat Push

When your opponent is holding you too close for other throws, the throat push is most effective, but it can also be a surprise move during grappling and wrestling matches. Jam your thumb into the side of the opponent's neck, pushing upwards towards their chin with all five fingers. Once you've pushed hard enough to create an opening between you and the opponent, use your other arm to push them back or off balance.

This move is difficult to execute without proper timing, but it is very useful against opponents unwilling to break the clinch or hold you too tight. It is also a great diversion tactic against opponents who think they have you cornered.

11. Hip Toss

The hip toss is a basic throwing technique effective against larger, stronger, or heavier opponents. Bend over and latch onto the opponent's shoulders with both arms to lift them from the ground. Once you've secured your grip, thrust your hips forward, forcing them upward and forward over your shoulder.

This technique can end in various ways, including landing in an immediate side-mount position or back-mount position, depending on where you throw your opponent. Since this move is so basic, it's an easy technique for beginners to get accustomed to Sambo quickly. Like the leg trip, it is very effective when used at close range. It can only be blocked or countered by an opponent who is aware of what you are attempting.

12. Suplex

The suplex is a basic move that can be executed in several ways depending on your preferences and the wrestling style you compete under. Pull your opponent up, lock your hands behind their head, and then fall backward, lifting them off the ground. It can also be executed by gripping lower on the torso and lifting them straight into the air.

Suplex

The suplex is regarded as a high-skill move requiring significant strength, balance, agility, and coordination to perform effectively. It is a great technique for beginners to practice against larger opponents, but it requires significant skill and training to execute properly.

13. Knee Pull

The knee pull is a beginner-friendly technique to stop opponents from completing their takedowns. Grip your opponent's torso or shoulder, and quickly drop down into a squatting position before sliding one of your knees between their legs. When in this position, stand and lock your hands behind their back.

This technique is used to sweep an opponent off their feet or trip them up extremely quickly. It's commonly used as a counter move to leg trips, but it can also be used if you are being held against the ropes by your opponent during wrestling matches.

14. Drop Toe Hold

The drop toe hold is another basic technique to take an opponent off their feet. Stand in front of your opponent and trap one or both of their legs between your thighs. Grab them around the back of the head with both arms. In this position, lean forward while keeping a tight grip on their head and shoulders.

This move can take your opponent down in several ways, depending on how you've caught them by the shoulders. If they are holding onto the back of your body or legs, trap one of their arms behind their back while turning around, facing away from them. If they are holding onto your hips or lower thighs, trap their arms behind you while falling to the tatami. This move is great for beginners because it's easy to learn and simple to execute. It also provides incredible control over your opponent when executed against larger, stronger opponents.

15. Four-Point Takedown

The four-point takedown is a versatile technique to ground opponents quickly. Drop down into a squatting position next to one of your opponent's legs. Wrap your arm around the back of their knee. Simultaneously grip the inside of their opposite thigh with your other hand. Stand and toss or sweep them onto their back.

This technique is regarded as a high-skill maneuver requiring much strength and training to master, but it's an excellent technique for beginners to get used to the Sambo basics. It can be countered with some effort by experienced opponents, but they will have difficulty stopping it from being executed properly.

There are many different Sambo throwing techniques to take your opponent off their feet. These moves are most often used in real-life situations when grappling against an opponent to avoid being struck or taken hostage. Beginners must practice with a partner before attempting these techniques in competition, but they can provide a significant advantage over larger, stronger opponents. Once you get the hang of them, incorporate a few into your training routine while getting used to Sambo matches. The more experience you have with these moves, the easier they will be to execute in a real-life scenario.

Chapter 5: Grip Techniques

Sambo is a Russian martial art that focuses on grappling and striking. Sambo provides an excellent background for anyone interested in MMA or self-defense.

One of the best aspects of Sambo is its extensive use of different grip fighting techniques. This chapter provides an overview of what a practitioner must know before effectively using Sambo's gripping system. Included are some tips on how to get started learning about gripping.

Sambo Grip Techniques Overview

Sambo has several grip fighting methods. Students don't have to learn all these grips. Rather, they need to fully understand their capabilities and be aware of their limitations.

The first grip fighting type in Sambo is called Shime Waza; this is a grappling resource in Judo and related arts. It involves using any limbs and body parts, isolating an arm or leg, and applying pressure to deny that limb's use or cause damage. An example of Shime Waza would be the standard armbar from mount. However, instead of using the legs to elevate the opponent's hips and create space, the head is used as the third point of contact.

The second grip fighting type is called Kansetsu Waza, also used in Judo and related arts like catch wrestling and Brazilian Jiu-jitsu. It involves isolating the opponent's arms and legs, pinning them to the ground, and controlling them to create an attack with maximum efficiency. An example of Kansetsu Waza is heel hook submissions from side control or leg locking an opponent who is standing.

The third grip fighting type in Sambo is called submission wrestling. This grappling is a blend of Shime Waza and Kansetsu Waza. Submission wrestling involves arm locks, leg locks, chokes, and pins to subdue an opponent or force them to forfeit due to injury. It is called "submission wrestling" because it doesn't feature groundwork or pinning methods.

The fourth grip fighting type in Sambo is called Combat Grip Wrestling (CGW). This grappling involves life-and-death struggles with an opponent where there are no rules, and the only way to win is by applying a submission.

Now that you have a frame of reference for the four different grip fighting types in Sambo, let's look at some basic gripping methods from each type.

Sambo Basic Gripping Methods

In Sambo, there are several basic gripping methods from which a practitioner can move on to more complex ones.

Georgian Grip

Georgian Grip

The first gripping method is the "Georgian Grip." Place your forward arm over the opponent's back and grab the belt or gi with your hand. The opponent's head is tucked under your armpit, and you lean onto their body for extra weight. The other hand grabs the opponent's sleeve. Various throws can be executed from this position.

Figure-Four Grip

Figure-Four Grip

The second gripping method is called the "Figure-Four Grip." To achieve this gripping method, grab an opponent's wrist on one side with your hand, grabbing their opposite elbow with your other hand. You control the arm by bending it at the elbow and pulling it toward you.

Figure-Four Reverse Grip

Figure-Four Reverse Grip

The third gripping method is called "Figure-Four Reverse Grip," To achieve this gripping method, grab an opponent's wrist on one side with your hand while grabbing their opposite elbow with your other hand. You control the arm by bending it at the elbow and pushing it away from you.

Turtling

Turtling

The fourth gripping method is called "Turtling" because the arms are used to cover the head, neck, and face. Wrestlers commonly use this grip with the over-under grip and during standup grappling exchanges. Pull your opponent's arms towards you while pushing your head into their chest. This allows you to pivot around them and take their back.

Combat Sambo Grip Techniques

Combat Sambo combines the four basic grappling methods with striking techniques to create an explosive and effective style. Stylistically, Combat Sambo resembles Mixed Martial Arts (MMA) for a good reason. The rules of Sambo competitions allow striking on the ground, and an opponent can win by submission or technical knockout.

Head and Arm Throw

Head and Arm Throw

The first grappling technique is called the "Head and Arm Throw" because the arm controls your opponent's head while you use your opposite leg to trip them. Grab an opponent's head with your hand and pull it towards you, planting your foot on their hip. Drive the side of their face into the mat and push down on their shoulder until they submit or fall over unconscious.

Russian Twist

The second grappling technique is called the "Russian Twist" because it resembles a submission you might see in MMA. Grab an opponent's arms while they stand and pull them toward you while dropping down into a prone position. Transition into a seated guard position and loop your legs around their head. Roll them onto their back or side, forcing them to submit from the pain of a joint lock.

Reverse Head and Arm Choke

The third grappling technique is called the "Reverse Head and Arm Choke." You pull an opponent's arm towards their neck while pulling on their head with your opposite hand. Grab an opponent's wrist using the inside of your arm and place it against the front of their shoulder. Loop your arm around their head and hold them in a headlock before pulling on both arms until they submit.

Turtle Guard Sweep

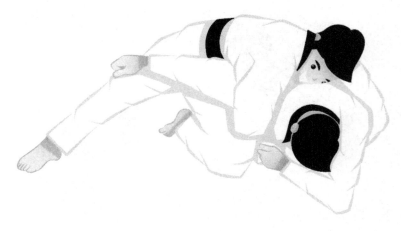

Turtle Guard Sweep

The "Turtle Guard Sweep" is the final grappling technique in Combat Sambo. This technique got its name because it resembles a turtle retreating into its shell. Grab an opponent's arms while they stand and pull them towards you as you drop down onto your back. Wrap your legs around their head and pull them to the side until they fall over or submit. This is not an easy technique but can be devastating if it lands successfully; end your opponent's winning streak with the Turtle Guard Sweep.

Leg Grips

When grappling in a Combat Sambo match, there is a good chance your opponent will attempt to apply these grips to your leg in an attempt to throw you. Here are some of the most common leg grips:

Triangle Grip

The triangle grip is one of the easiest ways for grapplers to pull a leg towards themself to execute a sweeping or throwing technique. Grab hold of the opponent's ankle and thigh before pulling the leg towards you. If you managed to pull them off-balance enough, you could execute a sweep while continuing with an attack to catch them off guard.

Single-Leg Slicing Grip

The single-leg slicing grip is exactly what it sounds like. Grab hold of an opponent's ankle and place the back of your neck against their knee before pulling them towards you. If they try to escape by stepping away from you, use this opportunity to execute a sweep or throw, allowing you to take control of the match.

Double Leg Grip

The double-leg grip is similar to the single-leg slicing grip; only you to control both of your opponent's legs. Grab hold of both ankles, placing the back of your neck against their knees before pulling them towards you. If they try to escape by stepping away from you, use this opportunity to execute a sweep or throw, allowing you to take control of the match.

Common BJJ and Wrestling Grips

When grappling in a Sambo match, there is a good chance you will encounter grips used by Brazilian Jiu-Jitsu or wrestling. Here are some of the most common grips your opponent will attempt:

Over-Under Grip

The over-under grip is one of the most common grips in Brazilian Jiu-Jitsu. Grab the opponent's wrist while simultaneously grabbing their opposite shoulder. Pull the opponent towards you until they are unable to move any closer.

Double Lapel Grip

The double lapel grip is another commonly used grip in Judo, Brazilian Jiu-Jitsu, and Wrestling. Grab the lapels of the opponent's gi and pull them toward you, shutting the distance between you. You will be in a position to break the opponent's posture and execute several throws.

Cross-Grip (or Under-Under Grip)

The cross grip is more difficult to apply than most grips but can be extremely effective if properly applied by an experienced grappler. Standing to the opponent's side, grab your opponent's wrist with one hand while reaching across their back onto their opposite shoulder. From there, pull them towards you until they are unable to move any closer.

Pendulum Grip (or Underhook)

The pendulum grip is similar to the over-under grip; the only difference is that your arms will be crossed over your opponent's shoulders. Grab one of your opponent's arms with both hands before pulling them towards you until they are unable to move any closer.

Lapel Grip with a Knee-In

The lapel with a knee-in is one of the most common grips used by Brazilian Jiu-Jitsu and Wrestling fighters. Grab your opponent's gi at the hips and simultaneously pull them toward you until they are unable to move any closer.

Other Gripping Techniques and Throws

Countless other grips and throwing techniques are used in Sambo competition, but they require a certain skill and dexterity level to pull off successfully. However, there are a few gripping techniques and throws that beginners can use to gain an advantage over their opponents:

Flying Armbar

Flying Armbar

The flying armbar is one of the best throws you can learn to use in a Sambo competition. Grab your opponent's right arm with both hands before pulling them towards you. Place a foot on their hip before jumping up in the air and simultaneously pulling down on their arm.

Leg Throw

This throw is extremely effective against opponents who like to grab onto your legs while fighting for control of the match. Pull your opponent towards you while sweeping one of their legs up and around. Then pull them towards you before moving your hips away from them to complete the throw.

Russian Hook-Sleeve Takedown

This takedown technique is used when your opponent manages to grab onto both of your sleeves at once, leaving you with no way to gain control over their waist or upper body. Pull your opponent towards you while pushing both of their sleeves in the opposite direction. From there, hook one of their legs with your leg before pulling them over and onto the ground establishing a pin.

Gripping for Back Control

This grip can be used when your opponent manages to get behind you, preventing you from taking control over any part of their body or even making contact with your arms or legs. Bring one arm over toward your opponent's back before grabbing underneath their waist. From there, slide their arm down across your chest, bringing it up to their neck and securing it against you for a choke or pin.

Sleeve Takedown from Standing

This move is used when your opponent reaches out and grabs your sleeves without having any control over your waist or upper body. It is a very common move in competition, but it can be avoided by turning away from it. Reach out to your opponent's grabbing arm and pull them towards you until they are unable to move any closer. Take their sleeve with the opposite arm and pull them down to the ground for a pin.

Scissor Takedown Method 1

The scissor takedown is one of the most commonly used throws in Sambo, but it can be avoided by keeping your distance from your opponent or positioning yourself behind them. Pull your opponent toward you by grabbing their sleeve and placing one of your legs in front of theirs. Scissor-kick your leg around them before bringing them down to the ground for a pin.

Scissor Takedown Method 2

This version of the scissor takedown can be used when your opponent stands in front of you with their calves against the back of your thighs, preventing you from gaining control over them using other methods. Pull your opponent toward you by grabbing their sleeves and placing both your feet on top of theirs. Scissor-kick your legs around them until they are unable to move anymore. Bring one of their legs over and push down on it with both of yours before bringing their torso down across your other leg for a pin.

Belt Grip Takedown Method 1

This first version of the belt grip takedown is used when your opponent reaches out and grabs the belt on the waist of your pants, preventing you from taking control of them from any other position. Place one hand onto their chest while grabbing onto their belt with the other arm and pull them down to the ground for a pin.

Belt Grip Takedown Method 2

This second version of the belt grip takedown can be used when your opponent manages to get hold of both your sleeves, preventing you from taking control over their upper body. Place one hand on their chest. With the other arm, grab the opposite side of their waist and pull them down to the ground for a pin.

Sambo wrestlers and submission grapplers can benefit from knowing how to effectively grip their opponents to make the most of every move they attempt. A competitor uses many techniques to grip and hold down an opponent. However, this chapter focuses on beginner-friendly takedown techniques to execute against opponents who have yet to develop an effective defense. These takedown techniques can also gain a significant advantage against opponents who are not expecting them, increasing their effectiveness. Sambo takedown techniques can be added to any BJJ or Wrestling game to improve your chances of successfully executing them against experienced opponents.

Chapter 6: Self-Defense in Sambo

If you want to take up any martial art, you must always know that mastering self-defense is an essential part of the process. It is especially true for Sambo, which we already know is a combat system providing weaponless self-defense tactics.

No one can depend solely on their ability to go on full-blown offense, throwing punches, kicks, joint locks, and whatever else they can think of. Practitioners can never succeed without mastering defense techniques, no matter how good or strong a wrestler or fighter is.

Learning self-defense proves beneficial even when you're not on the mat. Not only will you be able to skillfully and efficiently defend yourself against potential attackers, but learning self-defense also enhances your emotional, cognitive, and physical well-being in a plethora of ways.

Part of the self-defense learning process requires you to trust yourself and your abilities. The techniques you learn will grant you a great deal of awareness of your mind and body, which can push you to reach the limits you otherwise thought unreachable. You will also experience overall health improvements. These aspects will give you a confidence boost, automatically ameliorating other areas of your life in the process. Not only does great self-confidence boost your performance in the fighting ring, but it also helps you get that job promotion you know you deserve.

Every practitioner knows the key to mastering self-defense is discipline. It comes as no surprise that the level of discipline determines if we will succeed in any sport or area of life. When you're learning self-defense, you learn to avoid, withstand, and move on from attacks physically, mentally, and emotionally; this is generally a very useful skill in life. While life may not throw physical punches at us, it surely does have its fair share of obstacles.

Self-defense training also helps students to acquire the ability to set small and large goals and take the steps necessary to achieve them. Self-defense tactics are not easy to master. However, the process and how it's taught helps you learn to set goals for yourself and reach them even when they seem impossible. Everyone knows that success in life can't be achieved if you don't have solid goals.

When you're learning self-defense, it is never only about the current moment. Defense techniques encompass centuries of values, skills, and traditions. Think about everything an inclusive and comprehensive sport like Sambo has to offer. Knowing this, learning the skills doesn't only mean obtaining sufficient knowledge to execute them. However, the duty to constructively, properly, and responsibly use the skills is automatically passed on to you.

This chapter provides several tips on defending yourself against many of the throws discussed throughout the previous chapter. It also covers a few defense tactics for the submissions explained in the following chapters. You will also learn to defend yourself tactfully against someone with a weapon, including a step-by-step guide.

Sambo and Self-Defense

Sambo provides the most efficient and effective self-defense techniques among Karate, Judo, Boxing, and Jujitsu. Not only because it is a collection of their best moves but because it was designed to revolve around real-life problems, as well as struggles in combat.

Even if not on the battleground, law enforcement personnel require self-defense knowledge and skills to complete basic missions, like bringing criminals in for interrogation. Meanwhile, in combat and fights, individuals need an advantage over their opponents; for the Russian soldiers, Sambo offered that essential advantage.

Ultimately, Sambo is a combat system developed to purposefully gather only the best elements, moves, punches, submissions, kicks, sweeps, throws, trips, armbars, chokes, holds, and leg bars from various martial arts systems. Anything perceived as substandard was immediately discarded from this perfected system.

Real-Life Application

Sambo was developed for practitioners who needed to react to ever-changing situations immediately. It was for anyone having to incapacitate an opponent with nothing but the potential tools they already had, their hands, a chair, or a shovel. The system is developed to help its practitioners quickly disarm their opponents to minimize danger and make the mission as easy as possible. The purpose is to end a fight quickly, once and for all.

Although it was originally designed for Soviet soldiers, Sambo has become one of the best ways for the average individual to protect themselves and their families from the adversities of the modern-day world. Unfortunately, tragic incidents, such as robberies, assaults, and rape, have become quite common today.

Even more terrifying is the majority of attackers have weapons. So, learning self-defense techniques encompassing disarming strategies is necessary to guarantee safety.

With regulated competition, you know what to expect. Participants know which moves and elements are allowed, the time allotted (if any), and are aware of everything off-limits. However, no one knows what the enemy has in store in real-life struggles. Sambo teaches its practitioners how to act strategically in numerous situations, what to use against one or more opponent(s), and how to act if they're armed.

Defense Advantage

You might not recognize this unless you see it for yourself. Although, it's still worth mentioning that a perfectly executed Sambo move can incapacitate the adversary; this particularly applies to opponents unskilled in properly breaking falls. At this point, you can expect a fight to end because the human brain is not very receptive to losing touch with solid ground or a reference point. If the opponent doesn't position themselves correctly for the fall, their entire body will absorb the shock or energy. When you factor in the increased acceleration produced by leverage, expect the results to be disastrous.

As someone well-versed in Sambo self-defense, this gives you an incredible advantage. First, learning the proper falling techniques helps prevent this from happening to you. Moreover, if your opponent is on the receiving end, you can use their self-defense deficiencies against them, as mentioned previously.

Many people think learning Sambo is about learning leg bars and seizing the opportunity to get in a few throws. However, this is not nearly enough. Sambo is an entire system; those who have never practiced it think it is all about grappling and throwing. An avid Sambo practitioner knows that the proper execution of Sambo techniques requires extensive physical preparation and an understanding of leverage and the fundamental laws of physics.

Unique Execution

Sambo teaches you execution techniques for the most stressful and difficult situations. It teaches you confidence and helps you incorporate it into your technique along with speed; this is where Sambo differs from other fighting techniques. People think Judo and Sambo are similar, and the practitioners of either discipline can do both. Yet, few realize that Sambo wrestlers can make incredible Judokos, whereas the opposite isn't necessarily true.

This is why choosing the right Sambo coach is crucial. One rule to always go by would be choosing an instructor who is dedicated and committed to Sambo instead of someone who is a 3-time Aikido championship and a black belt Judo holder. Their success in other fighting styles doesn't mean that they excel in Sambo.

You don't have to dedicate your life to Sambo or practice as a competitive sport to become successful. You know you are a great player when you find all you have learned useful and can easily implement it into your everyday life. Think of Sambo as one extra survival skill or a toolbox that can perhaps save your life.

Defense Essentials

The best thing about Sambo is its collection of most combat styles. This aspect makes its practitioners well-prepared for various fighting styles without having to take up different fighting techniques separately.

Grip-Breaking Techniques

1. Technique 1

To break free from an opponent's grip, grab their sleeve with a two-on-one grip. Push their hand at a 45-degree angle away from your gi. This movement should be done forcefully and quickly while maintaining a good posture. Make sure to move your body in the hand's opposite direction. At this point, their grip should be loosened. Don't loosen your grip and continue to push their hand away from your body.

2. Technique 2

If the sleeve on your power hand is the one under your opponent's grip, bend your arm at the elbow. The slack on your sleeve is released as soon as you bring your thumb up to your shoulder. Then, lift your elbow, and yank your arm free from them and toward your back. You will be free from your opponent's grip as you pull your arm away.

3. Technique 3

Another way to free your power hand is by bending your arm at the elbow. Bring your thumb to your shoulder to remove the slack from your sleeve. Then, move your thumb, in a circular movement, toward the adversary's wrist and bring your thumb up to your ear. Forcefully and quickly pull away from your opponent.

4. Technique 4

A third way to free your power hand is by arching your hand to the back and grabbing the adversary's wrist. Straighten and round your back as you push down on their wrist to release the grip. Push their wrist as far away as possible.

5. Technique 5

If the sleeve of your lead hand is under the opponent's grip, place your power hand on top of their wrist and straighten your arm as you push your power hand downward. Their power hand should catch on their sleeve arm to release the grip.

Takedown Defense

1. Footwork

Prevention is better than cure. If the adversary can't touch you, they can't take you down. Everyone knows that great footwork is the essence of self-defense. For someone to take their opponent down, they must be within a certain range. By circling, using lateral movement, and being evasive, you can prevent takedowns from happening.

- Do not remain flat-footed

- Don't stop moving your feet

- Stay mindful of your low kicks, as they can throw you off balance

- Try to kick and punch as you remain in motion

2. Pummeling

If the takedown begins from the clinch, you will probably have to resort to pummeling. It is a common wrestling technique that helps you keep the opponent from throwing underhooks. If they manage to do so, they'd have plenty of leverage. Your goal is to pummel for underhooks, get in double underhooks, and finally disengage. In this case, you can perform a takedown.

3. Sprawls

Sprawling is an effective way to defend yourself against single and double-leg takedowns. You can use sprawls to prevent the adversary from grabbing you. It also helps prepare you for back attacks.

When the attacker approaches for a low takedown, push down on their neck, head, or shoulder. As you do, drop your legs and hips behind you. At that moment, your body weight should be below them. Aim for a headlock or choke in this position, or circle them to take their back.

4. Chokes

Although they are not permitted in several Sambo subtypes, you can use chokes to protect yourself against a hostile attack. But this is a risky strategy. However, it can end a fight immediately. You can go for a ninja, Peruvian, or Guillotine choke.

5. Throw Your Knee

You can throw your knee to stop an opponent from taking you down. However, in this defense strategy, timing is key. Either leg can be used to catch the opponent off guard. You'll have a moment before they decide to attempt another takedown.

Striking Defense

1. The Low Roundhouse Kick

Low Roundhouse Kick

If you are not very well-trained, do not aim for above the knee. So, this is when a low roundhouse kick comes in handy. If your arms are struggling, move your dominant leg back a good distance to get the maximum power. Make sure you're in a stable, balanced position and rotate your non-dominant leg's foot outward while moving your shoulders in the same direction. Then, quickly use your dominant leg to kick the opponent. However, ensure to raise your knee as high as possible before extending your leg. Use the upper back of your foot, rather than the side, to kick the internal or external side of your opponent's knee. If you hit the right spot, they will suffer excruciating pain and will not be able to resume the attack.

2. The Open Palm Strike

Open Palm Strike

Avoid using your knuckles during a fight if you are unsure of your abilities. Instead, use the open palm strike. Pay attention to the moment when your opponent leaves their face unguarded. Bend your fingers' upper phalanges, exposing your palm, and direct all your strength to the base of your palm. The ideal spot to target the blow would be their nose or chin. If you target their chin, you must blow it from the bottom upward.

3. The Ram-Elbow Strike

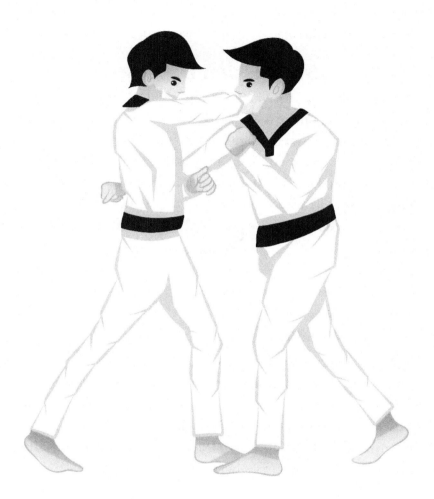

Ram Elbow Strike

Naturally, we are conditioned to protect our heads during an attack. If you're torn between covering your head and fighting for your life, go for the ram-elbow strike. If the opponent is going for your head, directing punches toward it, you must ensure your head is fully covered with your arms. Your elbows should be at the front, parted slightly to allow you to see. All your strength must be concentrated at your elbows, striking your opponent like a ram.

Target the blows at the upper arm's inner side or the nose. If you hit the right areas with the right amount of force, the opponent will be in great pain, granting you time to plan your next move.

Submission Defense

Avoiding it altogether is the best way to deal with a submission move. Therefore, timing is crucial. It doesn't matter if you're new to Sambo or have mastered self-defense tactics for years. How you act right before the opponent locks in a submission determines if you will tap or not. Don't wait until a submission is locked to start defending yourself, as this should be your last line of defense.

When you start practicing the sport, you will discover several things to consider before going in for a submission move. You must ensure you have the right grips, get the right angle, and, most importantly, open their defenses. This gives you the time and opportunity to act.

1. Kill the Angle

Several submission attacks require the opponent to get into a specific angle. For instance, if they're aiming for a triangle, being square to you makes it harder for them to complete the attack because the pressure on the neck will be faulty. It is the case with leg locks, armbars, chokes, and almost all the other submissions. If you can throw them off the angle before they attack, you're on the safe side.

2. Center Line Control

You must remember that you're at a submission risk each time you cross the center of your or your opponent's body. For instance, for opponents to execute armbars, your arm must be in their body's center. Controlling your centerline will keep you safe.

3. Lines of Defense

There are various lines of defense you can utilize. The first ones happen before the submission is executed, like killing the angle and controlling the centerline. You can also defend yourself during the submission, which requires you to hide your arms in the case of an armbar attack. Your last line of defense is when you're in submission, right before you are forced to tap. This is when you can execute an armbar escape or a hitchhiker. You can pull the opponent's knee if you're in a kneebar submission.

Defense against Weapon Attacks

Make sure the opponent isn't looking, or don't make any sudden movements if they're looking or aiming at you.

1. Only attack if they're 5 to 10 feet away from you.

2. Duck out of the barrel's sight and move to the exterior side of the gun.

3. Whatever you do, don't move closer to the attacker's chest.

4. Use your dominant hand to chop down or strike the opponent's wrist to disarm them. You can also punch the outside of their wrist.

5. The chances are that the gun will fly out of their hand. In this case, quickly reach for it or push it as far away as possible.

6. If they still have the gun, quickly grab their wrist to stop them from shooting you. Grip their arm as strongly as possible.

7. Pull their armed wrist away and down to the ground. Move it in a circular motion to throw them off balance

8. Finally, twist their arm. They will probably drop the gun. If not, you can easily pull it away.

Similar to when you're in offense mode, you need intense movement to excel in self-defense. While it looks like you're learning just one fighting discipline or style, your approach differs widely depending on which end of the fight you're on. With self-defense comes an entirely different fitness routine your body will surely benefit from. You'll also be able to keep yourself safe during unfortunate situations.

Chapter 7: Offensive Rolls and Strikes

Rolls and strikes in the Sambo arsenal are crucial. Strikes are a very efficient way to put an opponent on the defensive and can be used as a setup for a high-scoring throw or takedown attempt. When thrown from standing, strikes also allow you to keep your body close to your opponent, making it difficult for them to defend against throws or trips you might attempt.

On the other hand, rolls are an offensive technique. Rolling is similar to tumbling. However, some additional rules in Sambo prevent flips and twists from being thrown at full strength. For example, if you want to perform a forward roll in Sambo, you must maintain contact with the mat with at least one of your shoulders. Also, as with takedowns, the direction of your roll is guided by the shoulder that makes first contact with the mat.

This chapter breaks down some fundamentals of Sambo rolling and shows you a few variations that can be used as an offensive technique. There are more complex rolls with plenty of potential for variation, which is discussed later in the book.

The Basics of Rolls

Before we can discuss the different variations of rolls, it's important to understand the basic mechanics of a roll. There are two ways for a competitor to perform a forward roll in Sambo:

- Lead with your head and shoulder
- Lead with your hips and keep your legs behind you

The first option is generally safer as it protects your head from an opponent kicking or kneeing you in the face. However, it has its disadvantages. If you do not turn your head while rolling, you will end up upside-down and completely vulnerable to attacks.

You must be familiar with the switch-stance transition concept to be able to lead with either shoulder when performing a forward roll in Sambo. A switch-stance transition is when you switch your dominant stance while moving in the opposite direction. It is commonly seen in most martial arts with strikes, like punching or kicking, as the strike is thrown from one stance but lands in another.

Leading with your hips and keeping your legs behind you is slightly more complex, but it's generally considered the best option for a forward roll in Sambo. It provides great momentum going into the roll and is good protection from strikes and takedowns from your opponent. Even if you lose contact with the opponent while performing this roll, you are still protected by your legs.

The most popular roll in Sambo is the forward roll. It is used to get behind your opponent quickly without running, which is crucial for any approach that requires attacking from a standing position. Here are a few points when performing a forward roll:

- Keep your back straight and extend your legs as far as possible.
- As soon as you start rolling, push off the mat with your hands and thrust your hips upward.

- Roll as far as possible, keeping your back straight the entire time.

- Keep rolling until you make contact with your opponent or reach a safe distance from him.

Other Offensive Rolls in Sambo

The Backward Roll

Backward Roll

The backward roll is not often used in Sambo, but it is still important to learn and master. For example, if you are near the edge of the mat during a match getting behind your opponent using a backward roll can be very useful if combined with an aggressive standup game. Here are some key points to know when performing this technique:

- Keep your legs and arms straight but not locked out.

- During the backward roll, keep your head tucked in and faced away from your opponent.

- If you need to change direction or stop the roll before it is finished, quickly plant both hands onto the mat and use them to redirect yourself.

As with forwarding rolls, backward rolls are started by pushing off the mat with your hands. However, you must push yourself away from your opponent instead of toward him. Once you complete the roll and want to return to a standing position, use both arms to push yourself up.

When throwing a strike during an offensive roll, remember it might take considerable time to complete your roll and return to a neutral position. Depending on the situation, this could be dangerous since it allows your opponent ample time to capitalize on your mistake.

The Head Snap Roll

When thrown from a standing position, this is one of the most popular rolls in Sambo. Its main purpose is to get behind your opponent while simultaneously moving him back, setting you up nicely for whatever follow-up technique you choose. Here are some key points to remember when throwing a head snap roll:

- Keep your legs bent and maintain tension on your legs and arms.

- As with other rolls, make sure the first contact you make with the mat is a shoulder strike.

- Upon making an impact on the mat, immediately thrust both legs forward and up as high as possible to knock your opponent back.

The Sideways Head Snap Roll

This variation of the head snap roll is very useful if you want to strike your opponent with your shoulder but also need to move him slightly away from you. Since it starts and finishes in a different position than the original head snap, it can also move your opponent sideways if necessary. Here are some key points when throwing this variation:

- Once again, keep your legs bent and maintain tension throughout the roll.

- Thrust both legs forward while simultaneously pulling your head back with all your might.

- Aim to put your shoulder squarely on the mat, so it becomes the first point of contact.

- Once the shoulder strike is made on the mat, thrust your legs forward and up to knock your opponent back.

The Knee Slider Roll

This Sambo roll is similar to a bicycle or kip-up because it uses the momentum from the legs while pushing off the mat to return to a standing position. The knee slider roll is useful because it does not waste time getting you back up again, allowing you to turn the momentum of the match in your favor quickly. Here are some key points when throwing this variation:

- Make sure your feet stay as close as possible to the mat during the roll.

- Kick your legs out and up as soon as possible, as if you are trying to sit on a chair directly behind you.

- Once your back touches the mat, immediately thrust both legs forward so that they help push you off it.

The Fireman Roll

This is another variation of the Sambo roll used to strike your opponent with your shoulder. It is very similar to the original head snap, but instead of thrusting both legs forward, kick them out and immediately bring them back in. This is useful if you need to move slightly away from your opponent after the roll. Here are some key points when throwing this variation:

- Once again, maintain tension in your legs throughout the roll.

- Keep your feet as close to the mat as possible until they kick out and return to it.

- Thrust both your legs forward once you hit the mat to knock your opponent back.

The Cross-Knee Head Snap Roll

There are so many variations of the head snap roll that it would be nearly impossible to list them all. However, this cross-knee head snap roll is unique because you tuck your knee up so you can grab onto it once you hit the mat. It is useful if you need to transition from one dominant position into another on the ground to regain dominance. Here are some key points when throwing this variation:

- Bring your leg up, so it's parallel to the floor once you hit the mat.

- When you make contact with the mat, use both hands to grab onto your knee right above the kneecap.

- Thrust both legs forward to help force your opponent down once you begin to stand up.

The Ankle Pick Head Snap Roll

Another great variation of the head snap roll is this ankle pick variation that allows you to maintain dominance while transitioning into a dominant position. This roll is very useful if your opponent tries to put his leg down as you attempt to stand up from the mat. Here are some key points when throwing this variation:

- Keep a wide base with both hands and feet to maintain balance throughout the roll.

- As soon as your head snaps back, grab onto your opponent's ankle with one hand.

- Use your other hand to prevent your opponent from using his hands to stand (which will probably be in a defensive position).

- Immediately after grabbing the ankle, use both hands and feet to stand.

The Single-Leg Body Hook Head Snap Roll

This is another variation of the head snap roll that uses only one leg to keep you balanced throughout the entire roll. It is particularly useful if your body feels far away from your opponent's leg, making it difficult to grab his ankle with both hands. Here are some key points when throwing this variation:

- Maintain as much balance as possible on one leg throughout the roll.

- Keep your other knee bent and ready to hit the mat hard.

- Use both hands to grab your opponent's ankle once you hit the mat.

- Roll back so your head snaps away from him, and immediately use both hands and one foot to stand up into a dominant position.

Sambo Strikes

Sambo is a full-contact martial art allowing you to use submissions, throws, takedowns, and strikes to knock out an opponent completely. The best part about Sambo strikes is that they are very simple yet effective. Here are some of the most popular Sambo strike techniques you should know:

The Jab

The Jab

In Sambo, a jab is a straight punch supported by your front leg. In BJJ, it's a front snap kick since your leg usually bends at the knee to get more power on your strike. A proper Sambo jab can be thrown at long or medium distances, meaning you can throw it while standing or on the ground. Here are some key points when throwing this variation:

- Bring your left shoulder back slightly to get more power on your punch.

- Lift your front leg just enough so that it's parallel to the floor for better balance.

- Your front foot should be turned outward slightly (referred to as Franklin Stance).

The Cross

The cross is simply a straight right punch, but it's thrown with your rear leg instead of your front leg, like in the jab. Since this one is thrown at a long distance, it can only be used on the ground. Here are some key points when throwing this variation:

- Follow through with your punch so your shoulder ends up in front of you.

- Your front foot should be turned inward slightly for better balance.

- Use your rear leg to lift your front leg just enough so it's parallel to the ground.

The Hooks

A hook is a roundhouse kick that can come from the inside or outside of your body. For example, if you throw an inside hook, your body should be turned so that your front leg is closer to the target. Alternatively, if you throw an outside hook, your body should be turned so that your front leg is further away from the target. Here are some key points when throwing this variation:

- Keep your leg as close to the ground as possible so that you can pull it back quickly if needed.

- Throw your hook with the ball of your foot to generate more power.

- Rotate your entire body with this kick for better balance.

The Knee Strike

Knee Strike

The knee strike is a straight punch with your knee instead of your hand. This strike can be extremely effective, especially on the ground. Here are some key points when throwing this variation:

- Keep your knee bent while turning your body slightly to make yourself a smaller target.

- Lean forward slightly so you can hit your opponent with the top of your knee instead of the bottom part.

- Use your rear leg to lift your front leg just enough so that it's parallel to the ground.

The Ax Kick

Ax Kick

An ax kick is a roundhouse kick with your rear leg. This strike can be thrown at long or medium distances, so it can only be used on the ground or standing. Here are some key points when throwing this variation:

- Hold your front leg just enough to be off the ground at a 45-degree angle.

- Keep your rear leg bent and lift the front of your foot so you can strike with the ball of your foot.

- Lean back slightly so your weight is on your rear leg instead of the front leg to generate more power.

The Uppercut

An uppercut is a straight punch thrown at close range that comes up from below. You can throw a punch at your opponent's ribs, chin, or abdomen (if you want to put him away fast). Here are some key points when throwing this variation:

- Keep your knees bent for better balance.

- Tuck your chin to reduce the chances of getting hit.

- Keep your hands up for protection.

The Front Kick

A front kick is a push kick with your front leg. The ball of your foot is used to generate more power. This strike can only be thrown when standing since it requires good balance and flexibility in the front leg. Here are some key points when throwing this variation:

- Keep your hands up to protect yourself while turning your body slightly to make yourself a smaller target.

- Keep your hands up while kicking with the ball of your foot for extra balance.

- Bend your front leg slightly for better balance.

Sambo is a Russian martial art and combat sport where a fighter uses a combination of grappling and striking attacks to defeat an opponent. Several tactics, including throws, locks, strikes, and joint-breaking maneuvers, are used to set up an arm or leg of a submission technique. You need good flexibility in the ipsilateral hip, knee, and ankle areas to perform forward rolls effectively. Additionally, forward rolls can be used from several positions on the ground, like when flat on your back or sitting up. If you want to add variation to one of the strikes explained above, you can use a combination of taekwondo roundhouse kicks. These attacks are extremely efficient and stylish. Good luck.

Chapter 8: Upper Body Submissions

Submissions play a critical role in Sambo since they subdue your opponent in the game. Different submission techniques can be applied to exert pressure and pain on the opponent to make them submit or surrender. This chapter focuses on neck cranks, chokes, and arm submissions. It also explains how to apply each submission and why it is effective.

List of BJJ Submissions

Submissions constitute a key component of Brazilian Jiu-Jitsu (BJJ) and provide an instant feeling of accomplishment and victory to those who subdue their opponents. The art of submission is still evolving and involves different forms from other arts like Judo and wrestling. The following are some of the popular upper body submissions, including chokes, joint locks, strangles, and cranks. These submissions are performed from different positions.

Chokes and Cranks

A neck crank (also called a neck lock) is applied to the opponent's cervical spine to cause hyperflexion, hyperextension, hyper rotation, or extension distraction. These submissions are applied through twisting, bending, pulling, or elongating the neck and head beyond their normal ranges of rotation. In the process, the submission will induce a choke, leading the opponent to submit.

Guillotine

Guillotine

The Guillotine submission is very versatile. The practitioner can use it to compress the opponent's neck from a close position. It is the first submission learned by white belt students and can be performed from various positions. Some positions you can consider undertaking this submission include open guard, mount, standing, gi, and No-Gi applications. You can choose the appropriate position depending on what you want to achieve.

Rear Naked Choke

Rear Naked Choke

This choke is Gi and No-Gi and involves a common grappling submission where you compress the opponent's neck from behind to immobilize them. You use both forearms to perform the rear-naked choke, usually from back control. You have more control when you are behind your opponent, and you can use your feet and hands for maximum balance and effectiveness. The rear-naked choke is also called, among others, the naked strangle.

Triangle Choke

Triangle Choke

The triangle choke involves grappling submission, using your legs and the opponent's arm to execute. The triangle choke originated from Judo but has since become a popular BJJ submission. You can perform the submission from various positions, including the gi and No-Gi settings. This move is versatile, performed from closed guard, mount, standing, half guards, back control, or open guards like spider and z-guard.

Bow and Arrow Choke

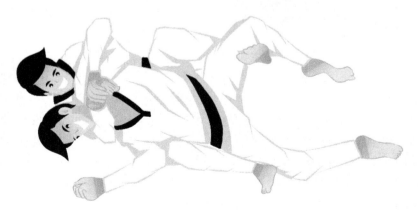

Bow and Arrow Choke

The bow and arrow choke involves the collar and is performed from back control. Use your opponent's lapel and a leg to finish the choke while controlling their movement with your legs. It is a Gi choke, and the name derives from the combination of two bodies during the choke. You can initiate this particular choke from closed guard, turtle, and side control.

Ezekiel Choke

Ezekiel Choke

This Gi choke is a sleeve choke. Wrap your forearms around the opponent's neck, and grip the inside of your sleeves for leverage. This submission choke is versatile and can be performed from your opponent's close guard, mount, back control, and side control. While choking the opponent, you have sufficient room to maneuver different moves out of harm's way.

D'Acre Choke

The D'Acre is another arm-triangle choke using your forearm together with the opponent's arm and shoulder. This Gi-based choke is similar to the Brabo choke that also uses the opponent's lapel. You can perform this choke from the turtle, side control, and half guard.

Cross-Collar Choke

Cross-Collar Choke

The cross-collar choke is performed when you grip your opponent's collar using both hands when they are crossed. Pull the opponent toward you and bend your wrist toward your opponent's neck crossing them. The cross-collar choke is very effective and is one of the submissions BJJ students learn because of how simple it is to execute. It has Judo roots like other BJJ submissions. The cross-collar choke submission is possible from different positions, including the mount, back control, and closed guard.

Baseball Bat Choke

Similarly, a Baseball Bat Choke is another example of a collar choke. Your hands grip the opponent's collar the same as gripping a baseball bat. Rotate your body while maintaining your grip, leading to a tight blood choke. Again, you can perform this choke from different positions like side control, bottom half guard, and knee on belly.

Clock Choke

Clock Choke

The clock choke is a collar choke against your opponent. Grab the opponent's collar and place your chest or hip on the back of their head. You can use this submission from side control or turtle, like other collar chokes.

North-South Choke

North-South Choke

As the name suggests, the North-South Choke is performed from the north to the south position. Use your bicep across the opponent's neck to add pressure on the head in this submission. Both players' feet are facing opposite directions. However, this choke can be challenging to finish because it requires finer details, so you must be very careful to avoid becoming the victim. The choke is often performed from side control.

Crucifix Choke

Crucifix Choke

This choke resembles the rear-naked choke, but the only difference is that it is performed using one arm from the crucifix position. This crucifix position looks like a Christian cross and is a back control. Wrap your legs around one of your opponent's arms and shoulders. (If the opponent is in the turtle position, this is when you can initiate the crucifix choke.) You can also use the crucifix choke to make the opponent submit using different armlocks. When you exert pressure on the arm, the opponent will feel the pain and quickly submit.

Thrust Choke

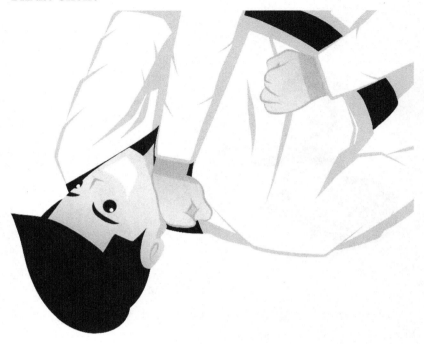

Thrust Choke

You can initiate the thrust choke as part of the guard pass or from the mount. Pull the opponent's lapel tight across your neck while moving your fist into the neck. Aim to exert more pressure on the subject's lapel so they feel the pain, making them relent quickly. You must be in the right position to execute this choke properly.

Anaconda Choke

Anaconda Choke

The Anaconda Choke resembles the arm triangle choke. Use your arms together with the opponent's shoulder to execute the choke. This move involves completing a rolling motion once you have established the grip. You can initiate this choke from an open guard or front headlock. You must choose the ideal position to execute this choke.

Peruvian Necktie

Peruvian Necktie

This is another variation of the arm triangle choke that you can do from the turtle position. Your legs must be on top of the subject's head and back to complete the choke.

The Japanese Necktie

Use your chest and arms at the back of your opponent's head. Also, use your opponent's shoulder and arm to complete the choke. This can also be a crank, depending on how you apply it. You can initiate a Japanese necktie from the turtle, side control, and half guard.

Loop Choke

Loop Choke

The Loop Choke involves a collar choke using your free arm to go behind the opponent's neck to finish the choke. You can use the loop choke as a counter to guard pass. Like other collar chokes, the loop choke is versatile and performed from various positions, including side control, open guard, turtle, and closed guard.

Step Over Choke

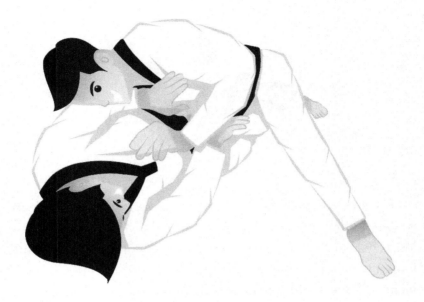

Step Over Choke

This choke is usually performed from the top side for control. Grip the opponent's collar and put pressure on the throat. Put your leg over the opponent's head to tighten the choke. You can initiate the step-over choke from the turtle or knee on the belly. However, you must be careful when performing this move.

Paper Cutter Choke

Paper Cutter Choke

This choke is a collar choke utilizing your forearm across your subject's neck. The choke is usually done using top-side control. This submission is sneaky, and many people do not anticipate or see it coming. To trick your opponent, consider using the paper cutter choke.

Gogoplata

Gogoplata

This is a rare submission using your hand and foot to create the choke around your opponent's neck. You must be flexible enough to wrap your leg around their neck and shoulder. Very few people can manage that feat with ease. You can perform the gogoplata in Gi and No-Gi, including different positions like mount, closed guard, and rubber guard.

Brabo Choke

Brabo Choke

This is a lapel choke often performed from the top half-guard. It requires you to loosen the opponent's lapel from the top and then grab its bottom. Wrap the lapel around your opponent's neck, changing the grips to complete. You can perform the Brabo choke from different positions, including the closed guard, half-guard, and side control.

Von Flue Choke

Von Flue Choke

To execute this choke, use your shoulder to push into the opponent's neck. This submission is usually performed when defending yourself from the guillotine using the top-side control. The way Von Flue Choke is applied often catches the opponent off guard.

Arm and Shoulder Lock Submissions

This section highlights different arm and shoulder lock positions you should know to make the opponent submit in combat. Likewise, these submissions vary, and you must take appropriate positions to execute them.

Monoplata

Monoplata

The monoplata is a shoulder lock you can initiate from a ¾ mount or mount. Use your legs to trap the subject's arm to complete the submission. This submission is versatile, and you can initiate it from spider guard, mount, failed triangle, and guard passing.

Americana

Americana

The Americana submission mainly targets the opponent's shoulder. To execute this submission, bend your opponent's arm and elbow in an upward direction while controlling your body and preventing the opponent from moving their arm. Americana submissions are versatile, and initiated from side control, mount, scarf hold, or closed guard.

Kimura

Kimura

Kimura is a BJJ submission originating from Japanese Jiu-Jitsu. Use both hands to push one of your opponent's arms behind their back. This action exceeds the normal range of motion, causing pain. Remember to control your body while simultaneously targeting the shoulder jointer. The submission was named after a Japanese judoka, Masahiko Kimura, who submitted Hélio Gracie leading to a broken arm. You can initiate kimura submission from side control, north control, closed guard, back control, and Z-guard.

Armbar BJJ Submission

Armbar BJJ Submission

The armbar is one of the oldest methods of submission that has existed for thousands of years. An armbar is a submission forced by exerting pressure on the arm at a specific angle to cause pain or injury. This submission continues to evolve and is used in different grappling practices. The armbar technique works the same way as you pull a lever. If you exert pressure on your opponent's elbow joint, they are likely to submit quickly.

You can perform armbar moves from different positions, like the guard and others. Performing this submission from the guard to subdue your opponent is the best option. You aim to grab the arm at the triceps and immobilize the opponent, preventing them from posturing. Your legs should also be in the right posture for easier control and to break their posture. Keep your knees firm as you perform the last steps of the armbar. The armbar submission is versatile, and you can initiate it from different positions, including mount, closed guard, side control, S mount, knee on belly, back control, turtle, and flying armbar.

Cutting Arm Bar

Cutting Arm Bar

This is another version of the regular armbar submission. Use your head and shoulder to trap your subject's arm and your knees to trap your opponent's shoulder. Complete this execution by exerting pressure on the backside of the opponent's upper arm. You can perform the cutting armbar from mount, closed guard, side control, and butterfly guard.

Bicep Slicer

Bicep Slicer

The Bicep Slicer submission compresses your opponent's bicep against your forearm. This submission provides easy positioning and can be used to counter the armbar defense. Bicep Slicers are legal in certain belt levels, particularly brown and above. You can initiate this submission from closed guard, side control, and Armbar defense counter.

Omoplata

Omoplata

This submission is a shoulder joint lock using your legs to trap and control your opponent's arms. To complete the submission, you must sit in a position to be able to rotate your opponent's shoulder past its normal range of motion, like the kimura. You can perform this submission from several positions, including the mount, closed guard, half=guard, and spider guard. There are also other variations of Omoplata, listed below.

- **Marceloplata** - This omoplata version allows you to finish the move if the opponent blocks your bottom leg.

- **Baratoplata** - This omoplata version is used when your opponent hides your arm.

- **Tarikoplata** - This is a shoulder lock version against the opponent that attacks with a bent arm.

Wristlock

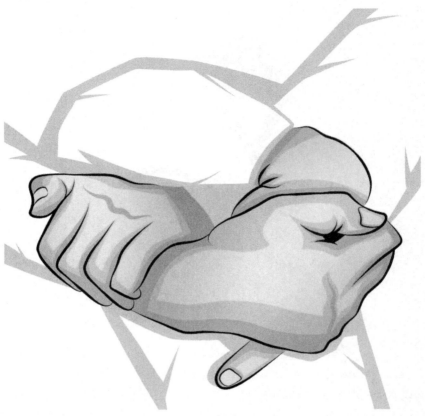

Wristlock

The wrist lock submission targets your opponent's wrist by forcing it to move past the normal range of movement. You can do this by rotation, hyperflexion, or hyperextension. To execute this submission successfully, immobilize your opponent's elbow and forearm first. Finish the action by forcing the palm forward or back, depending on your position. Wrist locks are versatile, and you can initiate them from different positions, including mount, side control, guard, and back control.

Calf Slicer

Calf Slicer

This is a compression submission. Place your forearm behind your opponent's knee, then pull the leg to compress the calf. This maneuver causes pain and leads the opponent to submit. You can initiate the calf slicer from different positions, including the turtle, half mount, truck, open guard, X guard, and knee on the belly. However, this submission is only legal for upper belts.

As you have observed in this chapter, several submission holds in martial arts are intended to subdue the opponent. The common upper body submissions include choke holds, compression locks, and joint locks, which can be applied from different positions. The next chapter focuses on lower body submissions and is required if you want to become a Sambo expert.

Chapter 9: Lower Body Submissions

This chapter focuses on the importance of groundwork and submissions in Sambo. As highlighted in the previous chapter, submissions help the participant to subdue the opponent. Here, we discuss the techniques of different leg locks, foot locks, ankle locks, and kneebars.

Leg Lock Submissions

Different leg lock submissions are available in Sambo, primarily based on exerting pressure on the muscles or joints of the legs. As a result, different leg locks come with different mechanical principles. Moreover, various leg locks have varying levels of success and are suitable for different situations. If the opponent's leg is trapped by two legs, it is extremely difficult for them to get out of the lock. Usually, submission is the only viable option to consider. The following is a list of lower body submissions you should know for games and self-defense.

Ankle Locks

Ankle locks are legal and used in competitions for each particular adult belt level. The ankle and the foot comprise a complex joint with about 26 bones, meaning several ligaments and bones can be damaged, resulting from the pressure applied under a lock. When you lock your opponent's ankle, they will feel pain and be immobilized.

Ankle Locks

An ankle lock is primarily concerned with causing torsion and hyperextension to the joint. Ensure you place your arms correctly around the foot. The bony part of your wrist must be positioned against the lowest part of the Achilles tendon, located above the heel. The palms should provide sufficient grip putting pressure on the tendons, leading to the opponent's submission if they cannot escape from the tight grip. When you apply this technique, you must ensure the opponent cannot easily escape your hold.

Toe Holds

A toe hold is a legal submission in Sambo, but you can only practice it at higher levels. For instance, brown belt levels or higher allow this devastating hold.

Toe Holds

The Toe Hold submission is primarily based on twisting mechanics. Use a figure four grip like the Kimura around the opponent's foot. Place your fingers around the pinky toe and twist in any direction, forcing it to exceed its regular movement. Pressure is formed when you squeeze the opponent's toe, causing great pain in the ligaments around the toe and making the opponent submit.

Kneebars

A Kneebar is a submission using your entire body power against one joint of the opponent, similar to an armbar. Tightly clamp down the opponent's leg to control its rotation. Apply pressure in the opposite direction of its natural bend on the knee you are holding. You will realize that your body position for a kneebar is similar to the posture you take for an armbar.

Your entire body must be positioned on the opponent's leg so your hips are above their kneecap. Also, consider other grips, like placing the foot in your armpit. However, these options are not as devastating. A kneebar submission is versatile and applicable from different positions, from the bottom, top, or standing. Additionally, kneebar submissions are legal for practitioners with lower ranks than the brown belt. It is one of the safest submissions to consider for different defense situations.

Heel Hooks

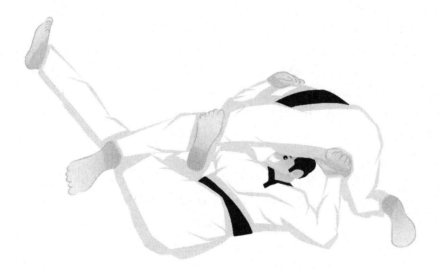

Heel Hooks

The Heel Hook submission is the leader in leg locks and is the most brutal. This technique affects the ankle and could easily destroy the knee's inner structure. Unless otherwise specified, this particular move is not allowed in all Gi competitions. However, it is a submission of choice for self-defense. You can perform the heel hook in two variations. The first one is the regular heel hook, and the second is the Reverse Heel Hook which is more dangerous.

However, both options share similar mechanics. Your opponent's toes are placed in the armpit, and the heel will be sticking out. Using one arm, cup the heel and place it under the thumb like the ankle lock. Pulling the heel using a twisting motion results in torsion of the knee and could completely tear most of the ligaments. When you undertake this submission, ensure you are in the correct position. Remember that this submission is illegal, so you can only use it for self-defense.

Straight Ankle Lock

The Straight Ankle Lock is known as the Straight Foot Lock or Achilles Lock. This lock is very common and uses your legs to control the opponent's leg. Apply pressure to their ankle and foot using your arms. Mainly two pressures will make the opponent submit when using the Straight Ankle Lock. The first involves the hyperextension of the ligaments and muscles above the foot. The second involves compression of the Achilles tendon at the back of the leg.

The Straight Ankle Lock technique forms the foundation for several other leg locks, like Toe Holds, Heel Hooks, and Steering Wheels. This submission also teaches you how to control the movement of the opponent's leg while using a safe mode of attack. Another important thing you should know is appropriate positioning.

Calf Crusher

The Calf Crusher submission, known as the Knee Slicer, resembles the Bicep Slicer lock, except you apply it on your opponent's leg, not their arms. However, the technique is illegal in many Gi tournaments up to the black belt level, like the Bicep Slicer. If – for some reason – you cannot complete the submission, it can transition nicely to the rear mount position. When you choose this particular technique, know your position to avoid mistakes that could backfire.

Figure 4 Toe Hold

The Figure 4 Toe Hold is a versatile leglock you can apply to your opponent's foot whenever you get close to them. You can use this submission as a primary attack. Alternatively, use this technique as a follow-up to other leglocks. The Figure 4 Toe Hold resembles the Heel Hook, but this one is a legal technique compared to other rotational leglocks. It means that you need to understand the situation to apply this technique and the action that follows.

Reverse Heel Hook

The Reverse Heel Hook submission is very effective, although it is illegal in most tournaments. Therefore, know when to apply this tactic. This submission is a rotational leglock that makes your opponent feel immediate pain and damage. With the flow of adrenaline, your opponent will quickly feel the impact of this technique, leading them to early submission.

Even if the technique is illegal, Sambo practitioners should still familiarize themselves with the Heel Hook for self-defense. If someone applies this to you and you cannot extricate yourself, early submission is vital to prevent severe harm to your heel. If you use the technique for training purposes, do it lightly so that you do not harm your training partner's ligaments.

Apart from the regular Heel Hook, the Reverse Heel Hook submission is worse and causes more harm. In Reverse Heel Hook, you rotate the opponent's leg outward instead of inward, causing a quicker submission. Likewise, you should not apply this technique during a training session. Also, know your limits when you use this particular technique.

Banana Split Hiplock

The Banana Split Hiplock is known as a groin stretcher, electric chair, and crotch ripper. This submission is an effective leglock that aims to attack the hips and groin areas. You can use this submission with other moves like foot locks and calf slicers. The electric chair variation uses the figure 4 leg lockdown position to control the action while the arms stretch out together with the other leg.

Leg Lock Positions

In different submission options, you should be in the best position for the best results. You cannot randomly use your legs without proper positioning since this could compromise your intended tactic. Using a leg lock to achieve quick submission might be ineffective due to a lack of control. Therefore, there are ideal leg positions you should know. Some submissions are attainable from several leg positions.

Ashi Garami

The Ashi Garami position is the best in the entire lower body submission system since it is controllable. This position stands for leg entanglement and is grounded in the Single Leg X Guard version. The only difference is the foot, which is kept on the butt in a single leg, now hooks on the opposite side.

Ashi Garami

The position also gives you control over the knee, hip, ankle, and correct grips. When you are in this position, you can completely immobilize the opponent, giving you opportunities for different attacks. The heel hook is the best submission option for this position, followed by the ankle lock. When the opponent tries to escape, consider the toe-hold alternative. This position gives you sufficient control of the situation and increases the chances of submitting your opponent. This position is legal, and you can use it in Sambo competitions.

Outside Ashi Garami

The Outside Ashi Garami is the second-best position for leg lock options. It gives you better control than the standard Ashi. Depending on the situation, you also have better transitioning options with this position. Regarding different mechanics, the bottom leg will remain in the same position as in the standard Ashi Garami. The top leg you use to hook the opponent's side butt in Ashi will go over the hip on the same side of the leg that is being attacked.

Outside Ashi Garami

Essentially, both feet are placed to the outside of your opponent's hip, giving you more control over the hip. However, you might sacrifice some control of the knee. The good thing about this position is that it gives you control of different movements. The ankle lock and heel hook are the most appropriate submissions for this position. Toe holds are also attainable from a top position in the same way as Ashi Garami. Kneebar is another short transition from the Outside Ashi Garami.

411, Honey Hole, Saddle, Inside Sankaku

For the ultimate back control position, the 411 is the champion of the leg-locking system. It offers you full control of various submission options to subdue the opponent.

411, Honey Hole, Saddle, Inside Sankaku

You create a triangle using your legs around your opponent's leg with this position. This triangle structure gives you ultimate control over the limb you are attacking. In other words, the 411 position means your legs should form a triangle shape between the opponent's legs. Keeping your knee around the opponent's hip fold emphasizes the position's power and pressure.

The opponent's foot is also placed across your body, opening the inverted heel hook. Some submissions in this position include ankle locks, toe holds, and kneebars. It is difficult for the opponent to escape from this position, giving you more power and control. However, the 411 position is illegal. It can cause serious injury, like knee reaping. The inverted heel hook leads to instant disqualification if you apply it in a BJJ or Sambo event. Therefore, you must be careful when using this particular position in regulated games.

Sambo Knot

Another name for the Sambo Knot is "knee reap," implying it is a dangerous position that can cause severe harm. This position is placing one of your opponent's legs in a triangle and keeping the foot on the leg under attack on the same side. You can control the other leg by locking your feet around the opponent's ankle, keeping it on the ground and bent. The Sambo knot offers effective leg-locking positions. You can do heel hooks and toe holds using only one hand while transitioning to 411 positions. The 411 position is illegal in Gi competitions, but apply it in self-defense.

Sambo Knot

50/50 Guard

The 50/50 guard position is legal in Sambo and falls between the triangle and Ashi Garami in control. The position forms a triangle but is outside the opponent's hip. The submission of choice for this position is a heel hook, although you can also use it on toe holds and ankle locks. However, this position's major drawback is that the opponent will be in the exact position as you, meaning they can also attack at the same time using leg locks, putting you at a disadvantage if you are not careful.

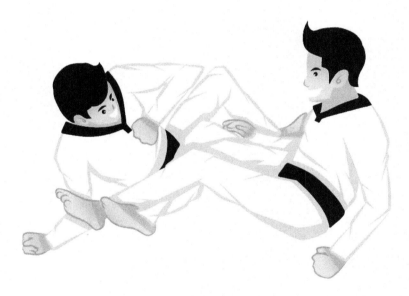

50/50 Guard

The Truck

The truck position was developed by Eddie Bravo and is halfway between the back and side control. It provides different submission options to the host. You can easily apply this position to the Calf Slicer and the twister. Choosing this position, you must apply to the submission you want to initiate. When you are in the correct position, you can easily read the opponent's intentions and take appropriate measures to counter them.

Different leg locks are safe, and effective submissions help you control and subdue your opponent. While other submissions are illegal, you should learn them for self-defense and only use them in those scenarios. Remember, not every leg lock works every time and against everyone. So, it is vital to know when to switch to another attacking system before it is too late. More importantly, you must be wary of the Sambo game rules to avoid penalties. The next chapter focuses on tips and measures you can implement to improve your Sambo skills.

Chapter 10: Improving Your Sambo Skills

This final chapter focuses on sharpening the sword and applying more advanced training to your Sambo skills. Once you know the basics, it is important to train daily by performing body conditioning exercises, repeated drills, and legwork practices to build a strong foundation. The upcoming sections discuss advancing your skills with daily practice providing much insight into structuring your training program from beginner to advanced levels. Considering the availability of expert Samba trainers, the possibility, methods, and effectiveness of solo training and training at home are covered.

The Importance of Daily Training

Daily training is important not only to master Sambo techniques and tactics but also to maintain your physical fitness. Exercise is a part of a healthy lifestyle and should be considered an essential component of your training.

Daily Sambo conditioning exercises will better prepare you for competition when you have to perform under pressure at 100% capacity with precise technique. Moreover, they prevent injuries by strengthening the ligaments and tendons that support joints like knees and elbows.

Daily drills train you to react properly from various positions, whether pinned in the mounted position, side control, the guard, etc., so when an opportunity arises during sparring or competition, your body knows what to do exactly.

Solo Sambo drills are an excellent way to develop your technique and practice combinations and attacks or counters without interference from another person. You can also use them as conditioning exercises for specific positions like grappling, throwing, pinning, mounting, back control, etc. However, you cannot master Sambo by simply going through the motions of daily drills.

A proper understanding of the positions and transitions is important, which can only be achieved by working with an experienced instructor or partner who will watch your technique closely.

The Importance of Sparring Drills (Sparring with a Partner)

Solo drills are limited in practicing footwork and motion. When grappling with a partner, you can practice moving around the mat and transitioning from one position to another until you perfect your form.

You cannot execute certain throws without first establishing an effective grip on your opponent's uniform or person – so it makes sense to practice your grips and throws.

Sparring drills (or "randori" in Japanese martial arts like Judo and Aikido) are the best way to master Sambo techniques through repetition. It's impossible to predict what your opponent will do or how they will react, but it is possible to train repeatedly under conditions that closely mimic a real fight.

It's easy to simulate the fight, but you must be careful not to commit or get injured fully. Sparring drills allow full-contact resistance while minimizing the risk of injury due to their controlled nature. Both participants know what is expected during each drill. They start from the same position, and the drill ends when one participant submits or is pinned.

Practicing Sambo techniques progressing gradually from simple to more advanced is important if you are training for competition. If your moves fail during sparring or the match due to a lack of experience and preparation, you must work on your weakness and gradually improve. Practice makes perfect.

Most techniques in Sambo are performed with a partner, whether during sparring or competition. Sparring or competition is not a solo activity. You cannot think of yourself as an island and go through the motions without realizing how everything fits together with your opponent's actions and reactions.

Body Conditioning Exercises and Drills

Sparring and competition are physically demanding activities. Therefore, it's important to keep the body in good condition by doing daily exercises that strengthen muscles, ligaments, tendons, and anything that supports your joints, like knees and elbows. Regular conditioning exercises will prevent injuries from occurring during training or competitions to continue improving your Sambo skills.

What Is Body Conditioning?

Body conditioning is about keeping your body aligned, strong, and flexible.

Improving your conditioning is the only way to prevent injuries and maintain a high-performance level during sparring and competition. Conditioning exercises are used in all sports for this exact purpose, not only Sambo.

Conditioning is anything that improves your physical fitness through mental or physical exertion.

Common Body Conditioning Exercises

- **Squats/Lunges** - Improves strength throughout leg muscles.

- **Power Skipping Rope** - Builds endurance through the use of lower body muscles.

- **Double Lunges** - Strengthens legs by using triple extension at the ankles, knees, and hips.

- **Exercise Ball Donkey Kicks** - Enhances workout for abdominals and buttocks.

- **Dumbbell Press Downs** - Provides a balanced workout for chest muscles.

- **Push-Ups** - Uses primary muscle groups to strengthen the upper body, especially pectorals (chest), anterior deltoids (front of shoulders), biceps brachii (upper arm), triceps brachii (upper back), and serratus anterior muscles.

- **Fighter Dips** - It's a very intense exercise, so it's best to start with low reps before increasing the number.

- **Weighted Pull-Ups** - Targets upper body strength in the latissimus dorsi muscle of the back, biceps (arms), and deltoids (shoulders).

- **Plank** - Strengthens abdominals, lower back muscles, and gluteus maximus.

- **Leg Raises** - Workout for abdominals and hip flexors.

These are a few of the many-body conditioning exercises that can be done daily. These drills will improve your physical fitness and speed up muscle recovery after training sessions, sparring, and competition.

It's important to avoid doing the same conditioning exercises every day because this can lead to overtraining and injuries due to repetitive motions. It's best to mix these drills to condition different parts of your body weekly (i.e., squats/lunges one day, power skipping rope another day, and so on).

Mental Conditioning for Sambo

Mental conditioning is as important as physical conditioning for high-level performance.

It's about maintaining discipline, confidence, and focus to succeed during sparring and competition. Mental preparation starts with setting goals you want to achieve within a certain time frame, then breaking these down into weekly or monthly steps so you can track your progress and enjoy the journey of achieving these goals.

Maintaining focus is also an important part of mental conditioning because it's one thing to set a goal, but you need to stay focused on that goal for it to be achieved. It takes discipline and patience, as some days will be more productive than others (i.e., you're focused and determined one day, but the next day you might be tired and unmotivated).

Avoiding things that could distract you, like listening to music or watching TV before training or competition, is also important. This distraction will change your mindset (music) or take away from the mental energy needed to perform your best (TV).

Other ways to improve mental conditioning include visualization, inserting positive self-talk into daily conversations, and setting rewards when you achieve weekly or monthly goals.

Visualization is imagining yourself performing each step of a specific task, whether competing or training, before doing the drill. It's a way to prepare for the task and, if done regularly, helps develop confidence in your abilities.

Positive self-talk is another mental conditioning technique where you look at yourself as a winner regardless of the situation (i.e., whether you win or lose). It means disregarding any negative thoughts that could affect performance.

Rewarding yourself for achieving weekly or monthly goals is a way to keep your motivation high. It can be something as simple as eating out with friends or watching the latest movie, but whatever it is, reward yourself after each milestone because this will help maintain focus on future tasks.

These are a few ways to improve mental conditioning for higher-level performance in Sambo.

Solo Drills for Sambo Beginners

Solo Sambo drills are very important for beginners because it's the best way to familiarize yourself with the basic movements in Sambo.

Here are some solo drills which should be done regularly by beginners:

Rock and Kick

The Rock and Kick drill is a great way to learn to move your hips to defend against an opponent's takedown or submission attempts successfully. It also helps develop hip flexibility, which is important for maintaining the guard position and transitioning into other techniques.

Technique: Lie on your back. Roll upwards, raising both your legs with the knees bent slightly simultaneously, creating a rocking motion. Repeat this movement several times to strengthen your torso and get accustomed to creating momentum with your lower body.

Kicking Up

This movement helps master guard techniques for triangle chokes, armbars, and omoplatas.

Technique: Kicking up is an extension of the previous movement. Lie on your back. Lift your legs to the ceiling together, simulating a two-legged kick. Go as high as you can. Feel the tension in your lower abs.

180 Rock

The 180 Rock drill will familiarize your body with angle change while on the ground. It is vital to master this movement so that you can pivot around the mat easily when performing your guard.

Technique: Again, start on your back. Roll up with one leg bent and the other straight so you are now in a sideways position. Keep both of your hands near your face for protection. Roll over and do a 180-degree flip using your head and shoulders as a pivot. Repeat this multiple times.

Rocking S Sit

The Rocking S Sit drill lets you quickly get on your feet after being taken down.

Technique: Lie flat on the mat. Roll up into a sitting position and stay there for one second before rolling backward to get back into an upside-down L-sit position (legs still bent at 90 degrees). Roll back to the initial position. Repeat several times before doing other drills.

Alternating S Sit

This drill simulates the movement of getting up on your feet after being taken down.

Technique: Start in an L-sit position, then roll to one side into an S-Sit before rolling back again. Repeat this motion several times for each leg. This drill will help you develop the strength and speed necessary to get away from your opponent's side control.

Gyro Drills

The Gyro drill helps you learn how to create small pivots on your hips, a very important movement in Sambo.

Technique: Sit with your legs bent and feet flat on the ground about shoulder-width apart. Lean back as far as possible, lifting both arms towards the ceiling. Lean your body to one side and then the other, moving from a full-fledged sit position into an L-sit with straight legs. Repeat several times for each leg before doing another drill.

Rope Pulls

This drill will help you learn to use your legs to stand.

Technique: Lie on the mat with arms stretched forward at shoulder height. Swing both legs upward toward your head, keeping them together (it is easier if you bend them slightly). Bring one leg back and then the other. Pull yourself forward. Repeat this movement several times to master it before doing the next drill.

Shoulder Rolls

The Shoulder Roll Drill will help you develop strength in your hips, which is necessary for transitioning between different techniques during a match.

Technique: Lie flat with arms stretched forward at shoulder height and legs spread apart. Roll forward onto your shoulders and then backward. Repeat this movement multiple times.

Tuck Front Roll

The Tuck Front Roll Drill helps develop speed while getting up and improving your transitions between different techniques during a match.

Technique: Lie flat on your back with arms stretched forward at shoulder height. Roll up into a sit position and then quickly roll back to get back in the initial Tuck Front Roll starting position.

Bridging

This drill will help you learn to use your hips to get up quickly.

Technique: Lie on your back, legs bent at the knee and close to your buttocks. Slowly lift your buttocks and get into a tabletop position. Your torso should be extremely stable and straight so that a cup of coffee can balance on it. Come back to lying down on the mat. Repeat this movement several times.

Intermediate and Advanced Drills

These drills are meant for experienced players. Make sure you master the basic skills before moving on to these more difficult ones.

Shrimping

The Shrimp Drill will help you learn how to get back on your feet quickly.

Technique: Lie on your back. Bend your knees and bring your heels closer to your buttocks. Rotate to one side, pushing your arms and legs as if you are pushing something away. Repeat on the other side.

Leg Circles

This drill will help you improve your footwork and coordination skills.

Technique: Lie on the ground, raise your legs, and draw imaginary 360-degree circles. Repeat the movement several times. It is an excellent exercise to strengthen your core.

Bridges with Leg Switches

This drill will help you learn to use your hips to get up quickly and improve hand-eye coordination skills at the same time.

Technique: It is a bridge drill on alternate legs. Get into a bridge position and balance your body only on one leg instead of both.

Keep alternating legs.

Crab Walk

The Crab Walk Drill will help you learn to quickly get back on your feet and improve your speed in transitioning between different techniques during a match.

Technique: Start in a sitting position with your legs extended forward. Keep both hands on the mat, palms facing downward. Lift your buttocks and move around the space in a tabletop-like position. However, you can keep your buttocks lower to the ground but not touching the ground.

Triangle Choke Variations

This drill will help you develop speed in getting up and improve your transitions between different techniques during a match.

Technique: A triangle choke is used when sparring. In this move, the attacker wraps his feet around the opponent's neck and wraps one of the opponent's arms in a leg wrap. This movement can be repeatedly practiced in a solo drill until it becomes muscle memory.

Quick Knee Cut

The Quick Knee Cut Drill will help you improve the speed of transitioning between different techniques during a match.

Technique: Start on your knees and hands perpendicular to your shoulders. Lift the left leg and the left hand and cut over to the opposite side by stretching your knee. Immediately go back to the starting position and repeat with the other leg.

Paper Mills

This drill will help you develop speed and improve your transitions between different techniques during a match.

Technique: Start in a high plank. Lift one hand and balance your entire weight on the other hand. Slowly move in circles, supporting your entire weight on one hand. Repeat with the other hand. Repeat a set on your elbow as a variation.

Bear Crawl

This is a great warmup and also increases core strength.

Technique: Performing a bear crawl is pretty simple. Get on your fours, hands perpendicular to your shoulders, and knees on the mat. Lift your knees and crawl around the area.

Exercises for Improving Balance

Balance is vital for improving your skills in Sambo. You will be thrown, grappled, and perform explosive and fast groundwork during sparring. This calls for a well-balanced posture and the ability to compose yourself in an imbalance quickly. So, you must train hard to achieve a balanced posture.

Here are a few exercises to help improve balance and posture:

1. One-Legged Standing, No Hands (2x 5 Min per Day)

This exercise is quite challenging for most people at first, but it improves balance and strength very quickly. You can challenge yourself by gradually increasing the difficulty, meaning you can gradually increase the time you can keep balanced on one leg without touching any surface for support.

2. Planks (3x 30 Sec per Day)

A plank is a simple and very effective exercise that strengthens your back muscles and is also great for posture since it trains your body to hold your back straight. The muscles responsible are often ignored but are very important in helping you maintain good posture at work or home.

3. Wall-Sits (2x 30 Sec per Day)

This exercise is simply sitting with your back against a wall and sliding down until the thighs are parallel to the floor. It trains your muscles to hold a sitting position that is "against gravity" for longer. If you're uncomfortable doing it against a wall, do it standing instead.

4. Neck Exercises (2x 10 Reps per Day)

This one's self-explanatory. Just move your neck in a clockwise and then counterclockwise motion.

5. Walking with Eyes Closed (5-10 Min per Day)

This is another exercise that trains you to focus better on balancing, so it's great for people who tend to get dizzy or feel off balance easily. Ensure to do it slowly and without distractions since it can be slightly dangerous if you don't pay enough attention to the environment.

This book has deep-dived into Sambo, compared with other martial arts. We have spoken at length about the various techniques, the essentials to get started, global competitions, and everything there is to know about this martial art.

In this concluding chapter, we spoke about improving your Sambo Skills using practice, group drills, and solo drills. The chapter also gives insight into a few drill exercises you can do to improve speed and transitions during a match.

Practice is crucial for achieving mastery in Sambo. Becoming an expert is not easy. However, it is easy to take the *first step.*

Conclusion

As you have observed, this book primarily focused on providing a practical and comprehensive understanding of Sambo and its critical elements like throws, holds, and movements. Sambo is a martial art that can be used for self-defense, and this book provided all the information about the basic moves. Before you consider using Sambo to defend yourself against an opponent, you must know how to execute different moves.

This informative book was carefully written to provide helpful details about submissions and throws. Many people have heard about the discipline of Sambo as a martial art, but the majority are scared of trying it. Indeed, performing different moves can be overwhelming to beginners. However, with the appropriate knowledge of the game, you will realize that everything is attainable. This book provided a step-by-step guide to understanding the crucial moves and throws to help you overcome the opponent.

Moreover, this book offered a basic understanding of Sambo and how it significantly differs from other martial arts. Martial art is a discipline that provides people with self-defense skills when facing threatening situations. There are different martial art styles, and each is designed for various purposes. However, Sambo significantly differs from other disciplines in several ways.

If you have a keen interest in Sambo, you should know its similarities and differences from other martial arts. The information provided in this book helps you familiarize yourself with the subject and prepares you for real action. You can significantly improve your skills when you have theoretical knowledge about Sambo. This essential book provided easy-to-apply techniques. Images are included to guide you as you learn to execute different moves.

You also got clear instructions from the book to help you understand the reason behind every move when practicing Sambo. Additionally, links for relevant videos are included to help you quickly grasp different moves you must familiarize yourself with. However, you need to follow the instructions laid out in the book carefully.

This book is unique since it is specifically crafted for beginners and those interested in Sambo. It is easy to understand, and all complex terms are explained in simple terms. In addition, the book is up to date and consists of information that might be new in the world of Sambo. It must be noted that this discipline has been evolving and is different today from how it was in its early days. Therefore, this book gives you the latest version of your favorite combat sport simplified.

It is great for beginners since it provides hands-on instructions to help them master different techniques quickly. While you need a teacher or coach to teach you Sambo, you can practice at home or with a sparring partner with the techniques detailed in the book. More importantly, the book is easy to understand, and you can execute various moves without seeking assistance from your coach.

We hope you enjoyed learning about Sambo!

Here's another book by Clint Sharp you might like

References

7 reasons to learn SAMBO. (n.d.). Retrieved from Sambo.sport website: https://Sambo.sport/en/news/7-prichin-zanyatsya-Sambo

Puncher Staff. (2018, September 26). What is Sambo? The Russian combat martial art explained Retrieved from Punchermedia.com website: https://punchermedia.com/russian-Sambo-explained

Rousseau, R. (n.d.). Russian Sambo: History and Style Guide. Retrieved from Liveabout.com website: https://www.liveabout.com/history-and-style-guide-russian-Sambo-2308279

What is SAMBO? (1483). Retrieved from Insidethegames.biz website: https://www.insidethegames.biz/articles/1045459/what-is-Sambo

Marc. (2021, May 15). BJJ vs Sambo: Key differences & similarities. Bjjsuccess.Com. https://www.bjjsuccess.com/bjj-vs-Sambo

Robert. (2021, March 15). Sambo vs judo: Differences and effectiveness. Wayofmartialarts.Com. https://wayofmartialarts.com/Sambo-vs-judo

Samhith. (n.d.). Difference between Sambo and wrestling. Differencebetween.Info. Retrieved

from http://www.differencebetween.info/difference-between-Sambo-and-wrestling

Super User. (n.d.). Judo Rules. Rulesofsport.Com. Retrieved from
https://www.rulesofsport.com/sports/judo.html

What martial art is the most effective: Sambo, Judo or BJJ? (n.d.).
Quora.Com. Retrieved from https://www.quora.com/What-martial-art-is-
the-most-effective-Sambo-Judo-or-BJJ

7 reasons to learn SAMBO. (n.d.). Sambo.Sport. Retrieved from
https://Sambo.sport/en/news/7-prichin-zanyatsya-Sambo

Does Sambo have a ranked belt system? What are the grades of each
Sambo belt? (2020,

November 14). Budodragon.Com.

https://budodragon.com/does-Sambo-have-a-ranked-belt-system

Requirements to the Sambo uniform. (n.d.). Sambogear.Com. Retrieved
from

https://Sambogear.com/en/pages/requirements-Sambo-uniform

r/Sambo - What does it take to be "Master of the sport" and is there an
equivalent in other

combat sports e.g. a 9th degree red belt in BJJ. (n.d.). Reddit.Com.
Retrieved from

https://www.reddit.com/r/Sambo/comments/93sv92/what_does_it_take_to
_be_master_of_the_sport_and

Sambo – Overview – Physicalguru.com. (n.d.). Physicalguru.Com.
Retrieved from

https://physicalguru.com/sports-games/Sambo-overview

Spot, B. (2017, November 23). How effective is the Sambo? Bjj-
Spot.Com. https://www.bjj-spot.com/how-effective-is-the-Sambo

What are the course fees of Mixed Martial Arts training? (n.d.).
Quora.Com. Retrieved from https://www.quora.com/What-are-the-course-
fees-of-Mixed-Martial-Arts-training

Fanatics Authors. (n.d.). Top 5 Sambo Fusion Grappling Techniques for BJJ. Bjjfanatics.Com. Retrieved from https://bjjfanatics.com/blogs/news/top-5-Sambo-fusion-grappling-techniques-for-bjj

Kesting, S. (2021, March 1). Top 10 throws and takedowns for BJJ. Grapplearts.Com. https://www.grapplearts.com/top-10-throws-and-takedowns-for-bjj

lvshaolin. (2019, December 9). 9 judo throws every beginner should learn. Lvshaolin.Com.

https://www.lvshaolin.com/judo-throws

The core concepts of throwing techniques. (2019, November 28). Ymaa.Com.

https://ymaa.com/articles/2019/12/the-core-concepts-of-throwing-techniques

BJJEE. (2020, January 15). How to use the "Georgian grip" to set up throws in BJJ. Bjjee.Com.

https://www.bjjee.com/videos/how-to-use-the-georgian-grip-to-set-up-throws-in-bjj

Five Grips All Grapplers Need to Know. (2021, February 4). Gumacliftonnj.Com.

https://gumacliftonnj.com/five-grips-all-grapplers-need-to-know

Heroes, B. J. J. (2016, October 25). Most common Jiu jitsu hand grips. Bjjheroes.Com.

https://www.bjjheroes.com/techniques/most-common-hand-grips-in-jiu-jitsu

5 reasons you should learn self-defence. (2020, February 20). Retrieved from Com.au website:

https://shirudoselfdefence.com.au/blog/5-reasons-you-should-learn-self-defence

Barlow, T. (2016, November 23). Three key concepts to defend any submission. Retrieved from Tombarlowonline.com website: https://tombarlowonline.com/three-key-concepts-to-defend-any-submission

Evolve, M. M. A. (2018, May 26). How to break grips in BJJ. Retrieved from Evolve-mma.com website: https://evolve-mma.com/blog/how-to-break-grips-in-bjj

Kongling, M. (2021, February 23). 3 self-defense striking techniques everyone should know. Retrieved from 6Dragonskungfu.com website: https://www.6dragonskungfu.com/3-self-defense-striking-techniques-everyone-should-know

The 5 most effective types of takedown defense. (n.d.). Retrieved from Nymaa.com website: https://www.nymaa.com/announcements/The-5-Most-Effective-Types-of-Takedown-Defense_AE210.html

Vorobiev, M. (2020, July 6). Combat SAMBO for Self-Defense. Retrieved from

Firearmsnews.com website: https://www.firearmsnews.com/editorial/combat-Sambo-for-self-defense/378679

Ivanov, D. (2020, February 15). Does Sambo Have Striking Techniques? Mmaclan.Com. https://mmaclan.com/does-Sambo-have-striking-techniques

Ola. (2020, September 30). Striking in BJJ - all you need to know - BJJ spot. Bjj-Spot.Com.

https://www.bjj-spot.com/striking-in-bjj-all-you-need-to-know

Marc. (2020, September 7). 40+ Brazilian Jiu-Jitsu submissions you need to know.

Bjjsuccess.Com. https://www.bjjsuccess.com/brazilian-jiu-jitsu-submissions

Kesting, S. (2016, June 18). 37 powerful BJJ submissions for grapplers. Grapplearts.Com. https://www.grapplearts.com/37-powerful-bjj-submissions-for-grapplers

MMA Submission Holds - an online guide to mixed martial arts submissions. (2007, February 9). Mma-Training.Com. http://www.mma-training.com/mma-submission-holds

Armbar – BJJ submission explained. (2020, October 16). Lowkickmma.Com.

https://www.lowkickmma.com/armbar

MMA Wiki.org Staff. (2014, February 13). Neck Crank. Mmawiki.org.

https://www.mmawiki.org/en/neck-crank

Leg locks - positions & submissions - BJJ world. (2018, February 13). Bjj-World.Com.

https://bjj-world.com/leg-locks-ultimate-guide-positions-submissions

Downright Nasty Sambo Submissions For BJJ. (2020, July 25). Bjj-World.Com.

https://bjj-world.com/Sambo-submissions-for-bjj

Kesting, S. (2016, June 18). 37 powerful BJJ submissions for grapplers. Grapplearts.Com.

https://www.grapplearts.com/37-powerful-bjj-submissions-for-grapplers

Kesting, S. (2020, July 24). The ultimate guide to BJJ solo drills. Grapplearts.Com.

https://www.grapplearts.com/the-ultimate-guide-to-bjj-solo-drills

List of martial arts stretching techniques. (2018, September 7). Blackbeltwiki.Com.

https://blackbeltwiki.com/stretching

No title. (n.d.). Jiujitsutimes.Com. Retrieved from https://www.jiujitsutimes.com/intermediate-bjj-building-submission-combinations

Unsymmetrical grips in judo, sambo and BJJ.
https://forums.sherdog.com/threads/unsymmetrical-grips-in-judo-sambo-and-bjj.2823877/

Understanding Sambo https://matcraft.ca/blog/2018/2/13/understanding-sambo

Charles Gracie Jiu-Jitsu academy
https://www.charlesgracie.com/tournament-scoring-system/

Printed in Great Britain
by Amazon

42724184R00096